THE ADVENTUROUS CAPTAIN

The Life and Voyages of James Cook, R.N., F.R.S.

By
KEITH SNOWDEN

CASTLEDEN PUBLICATIONS
PICKERING

© *Keith Snowden 1999*

ISBN 0 9527548 4 3

First published 1999
Reprinted 2001.
Reprinted 2002

Typeset, Printed and Bound
at the press of the publisher
CASTLEDEN PUBLICATIONS,
11,Castlegate, Pickering,
North Yorkshire, YO18 7AX.
Telephone 01751 476227.

INTRODUCTION

Walk cheerfully over the world, answering that of God in everyone.
(George Fox, 1656.)

CAPTAIN COOK, for most of his life, can be said to have followed the spirit of Fox's instruction in that he looked for the good in everyone, though sometimes his trust was misplaced.

The visit of the Australian-built replica of the *Endeavour,* in 1997, caused great interest, but it was not a true replica, for it was equipped with an engine, refrigerator and other modern conveniences. James Cook had no such luxuries ; his ships were dependant on the winds, often at the mercy of them and the course they could sail was governed by the direction of the wind. Much depended on the ability of his sailors,
'Who toil for bread from early morn
Till half the night has flown'
as William S.Gilbert put it.

Captain Cook has been a subject that has greatly interested me from an early age, and various articles and books have fallen into my hands over the years. The contents of this little book have in large part been derived from Captain Cook's own journals and those of his officers. The nautical terms used are those which applied in his day. The names of many places have altered since his day, but for the most part I have stuck to his renditions.

Of his private life - what little time he had to himself - little is known, but his adventurous experiences on his great voyages of discovery are chronicled here.

K.S.
Pickering,
1999.

ACKNOWLEDGEMENTS
THE AUTHOR thanks the following who have assisted him in his research:
Mr E.W.Peel for his gift.
Mrs Catherine Sleightholme for the loan of her wonderful antique atlas.
Pannett Park Museum, Whitby, for permission to use the picture on page 60.

Charts and photographs by the author.

EARLY DAYS

WHEN James Cook, of Ednam, Roxboroughshire, Scotland, married Grace Pace, of Thornaby-on-Tees, in 1725, he would little realise that three years later he would become the father of one of the worlds greatest navigators. His third son, also James, one of nine children, was born on October 27th 1728, in a two-roomed thatched farm worker's cottage at Marton-in-Cleveland. Young James began his schooling at Marton, in a Dames school run by a Mrs Walker. When James was eight years old his father was hired to work at Aireyholme Farm, Great Ayton, the property of Mr Thomas Scottowe, the Lord of the Manor of Ayton. James senior built himself a cottage in Great Ayton, and James Junior attended the village school there. Mr Scottowe, greatly interested in the young James's development, paid for his schooling. Part of the curriculum was religious instruction, as well as writing and arithmetic. On leaving school, James engaged in farm work for three to four years, when Mr Scottowe secured him a position with Mr William Sanderson, a merchant and grocer at Staithes.

It must have been while he was at Staithes that James got the call of the sea, for after he had worked at Mr Sanderson's for eighteen months, he expressed the desire to take up the life of a sailor. Mr Sanderson consulted Mr Scottowe and James's request was suported, prividing the ship-owner had a good record for treating his men fairly, and who had a good religious background. John and Henry Walker, of Whitby, were Quaker ship-owners and their reputation was one of the best for honesty and fairness. Whitby was enjoying a boom period when James, now eighteen years of age, was hired by John Walker ; the trade in coal from Newcastle and alum from Mulgrave was flourishing. The ship-builders were busy making vessels to serve these trades.

John Walker lived in Grape Lane, Whitby, and it was agreed that when on shore, Cook would lodge in his master's house. This was mostly in the winter when insurance premiums were loaded for ships venturing forth in the winter months ; the Walker vessels remaining in port. It was for the last three months of 1747 that Cook sailed in the *Freelove*, a collier of 341 tons, built at Yarmouth. Coal was carried from Tyneside to London for eleven weeks, when the ship returned to Whitby just after Christmas.

After having been laid up for nine weeks, the *Freelove* returned to the collier trade with James Cook as one of the eight apprentices. After nine weeks the ship returned to Whitby, when Cook was engaged to help with the fitting and rigging of a new vessel, the *Three Brothers,* rated at 600 tons. Part of the fitting work included the provision of stables. After its maiden voyage in 1748, the new ship was immediately hired by the Government for transporting troops and provisions over a period of six months.

Cook rejoined the *Three Brothers* in April, 1749, when the ship was employed in the Norway trade. Cook completed his apprenticeship and sailed again in the *Three Brothers* until December 1749, when he left the service of John Walker. In the following February he sailed out of Shields in a ship named *The Mary,* with which he served until the October.

By February of 1750 he was back in the service of John Walker, rejoining the crew of the *Three Brothers,* until the July, when he was transferred to the *Friendship.* James was to remain in that vessel for five years, except for the times when she was laid up for the winter, or in Whitby for repairs. It was during those years that he was promoted to mate.

England and France went to war with each other in 1756, in what was to be known as the Seven Years' War. In Canada the French had a good relationship with the native North Americans, trading with them for furs, by exchanging a few trinkets. The English were not popular for they felled the forests, which were the natives hunting grounds. A small French settlement at the mouth of the Mississippi, which they named Louisiana, after their king and which they claimed as 'A New France' that should stretch west of all English colonies, securing the waterways by stockaded forts and, with the help of the natives, effectively shut off the English colonies from the distant interior of the continent. There had been some fighting in the past between the English and the French, and General Braddock had been sent to protect the English. He marched on until he came to the place where the French and the Indians surrounded him in the forest, and he and most of his men were shot down from behind the trees. After that there could be no continuance of peace with France.

It may have been the preparations for the Seven Years' War which decided James Cook to enlist in the Royal Navy, for in June 1755 he discharged himself at London and volunteered for the service at Wapping, 'Having in mind,' he said, 'to try my luck that way.' He entered as an able seaman on board the *Eagle,* a man-of-war of sixty guns, then commanded by Captain Hamer, but shortly after by Captain Palliser - Cook's warm and constant friend. During his two years service in the *Eagle,* the ship was engaged in

JOHN WALKER'S HOUSE, Grape Lane, Whitby.

TATE HILL PIER : Starting point for many of Cook's early voyages.

action off the French coast. Considering how best he could help the young man, who had served too short a term in the Royal Navy to obtain a commission, Captain Palliser advised that a master's warrant should be procured for him - this being a position for which, both from age and experience he was well-fitted. Masters in the Royal Navy in those days were appointed by warrant, and were generally taken direct from merchant service without going through any preparatory grade. A warrant was obtained and on May 10th, 1759, James Cook was appointed to the *Grampus,* sloop of war.

ADVANCEMENT IN THE NAVY

OBTAINING his Masters warrant, James Cook was appointed Master of the *Pembroke,* a ship of sixty guns, in 1758 to join English forces in Halifax, Nova Scotia. Sir Charles Saunders commanded the English fleet, which in conjunction with the army under General Wolfe, was engaged in the siege of Quebec.

Cook was now to prove his talent for scientific study by taking soundings in the channel of the St.Lawrence River, between the Isle of Orleans and the north shore, under the noses of the French in their fortified camps at Montmorency and Beauport. The object of this survey being to enable a landing of the army under General Wolfe. The operation had to be carried out during the hours of darkness, but the French got wind of Cook's presence and they laid a plan to catch him by concealing a number of Indians in a wood with their canoes. As the ships barge, in which Cook was making his survey passed, the canoes darted out and chased him. He made for the Isle of Orleans with a host of yelling natives furiously paddling after him. As they gained on him, Cook saw the English hospital, where there was a guard, and steered towards it, the bows of the Indians' canoes almost touching the barges stern. He sprang from his seat over the bow of the barge followed by his crew. The barge was captured by his enemy, which they made off with in triumph. Cook was able to carry out an accurate survey of the more difficult parts of the river below Quebec. With the help of Cook's charts the English fleet, by June was able to sail up the river and anchor off the Isle of Orleans. Quebec fell to the English on September 18th, 1759.

When the conquest of Canada had been achieved, Admiral Saunders ordered the larger ships back to England, following on himself in the

Somerset, leaving the command of the fleet to Lord Colvill. who had the commodore's flag flying on board the *Northumberland.* On September 22nd, Cook was appointed Master, by warrant from his lordship.

As the squadron wintered at Halifax, Cook employed the leisure which the winter afforded him in gaining knowledge, much as he had done in the attic of John Walker's house at Whitby during his apprenticeship, and which was to stand him in good stead for his future role in life. He began to study astronomy and science. In 1760 he was promoted to the rank of lieutenant as a reward for his services.

In 1762, still with the *Northumberland,* Cook was engaged in the recapture of Newfoundland. The efforts made by Cook in surveying the harbour and heights came to the notice of the acting governor, Captain Graves, who, getting to know Cook, formed a very high opinion of him. Cook returned to England at the end of the year, and on December 21st, he married Elizabeth Batts at Barking, in Sussex. He had been engaged to this lady for some time. Although she would see little enough of him, she bore him six children, three of whom died in their infancy.

Shortly after Cook's marriage, a peace treaty was signed between France and Spain, following which, Captain Graves was appointed Governor of Newfoundland. As the island was of great importance to England, he asked for an establishment for a survey of its coasts, offering the direction of it to James Cook. With some reluctance the government agreed. In 1764, Sir Hugh Palliser was made Governor of Newfoundland and Labrador. Cook was appointed Marine Surveyor of the Province, and the schooner *Grenville* was placed under his command. Apart from his thorough survey of the coast, Cook penetrated into the interior of the country, discovering some lakes hitherto unknown.

On August 5th, an eclipse of the sun occurred and Cook made an observation of it from one of the Burgeo Islands, near the south-west of Newfoundland. He wrote a paper on it which was published in the *Philosophical Transactions of the Royal Society.* His last visit to Newfoundland as a marine surveyor was in 1767. His charts of the coastline had served to inform the government as to the value of Newfoundland, so that when drawing up articles of peace with France, to assist on arrangements which secured Great Britain the advantages which its coast afforded.

THE VOYAGE OF THE ENDEAVOUR

BEFORE James Cook started on his first great voyage of discovery, at the instigation of King George III, two expeditions were fitted out to circumnavigate the globe. Commodore Byron commanded the *Dolphin* and the *Tamer,* sailing from the Downs on June 21st,1764. Having visited the Falkland Islands, he sailed into the Pacific Ocean, where he discovered a number of islands ; returning to England on May 9th,1766. The following August the *Dolphin* was sent out again under the command of Captain Wallis, with the *Swallow,* under Captain Cartaret. Proceeding together at first, they were separated at the west end of the Straits of Magalhaens. Wallis sailed more westerly than any previous navigator in so high a latitude, but met with no land until he got within the tropics. He returned to England in May,1768.

Captain Carteret discovered five islands as well as the Straits between New Britain and New Ireland, returning to England in March,1769.

That year of 1769 was to see the transit of the planet Venus over the suns disc. At the beginning of the previous year the Royal Society presented a memorial to the king setting forth the advantages to be derived from accurate observations of this phenomenon in different parts of the world, in particular from a southern latitude. The Admiralty were directed by the king to provide a proper vessel for this purpose. James Cook was to command the ship, with Mr Charles Green, the astronomer, to make observations.

A collier, built at Whitby by Thomas Fishburn, and owned by Captain Thomas Millen, of Whitby, and named the *Earl of Pembroke,* was chosen for the expedition. The ship was three years old when the Admiralty procured her and renamed her the *Endeavour.* Visitors to the Australian-built replica on her visit to England in 1997, were amazed to find how small the ship was, being little more than 100 feet in length, and found it hard to conceive that a total personnel of 94, plus provisions, supplies and equipment could be accommodated in so small a vessel. Although larger ships were built by Fishburn, their size was limited by the narrow passage between the mouth of the Esk and the outer harbour. Whitby colliers were usually between 350 - 500 tons.

Cook had as his second in command Lieutenant Zachary Hicks and John Gore ; the second mate was Charles Clerke and the surgeon was Mr Monkhouse. Dr Solander was a Linnean botanist and Mr Buchan was the

ENDEAVOUR WHARF, Whitby, Site of the shipyard where Cook's vessels were built.

A TYPICAL THREE-MASTER

draughtsman. Joseph Banks, whom Cook described 'of ample fortune,' volunteered to go, taking with him a secretary and two artists.

Captain Wallis returned from his expedition and expressed his opinion that a harbour he had discovered and called King George Island, would be a suitable spot for the observation of the transit of Venus to be made. This was to be Cook's first destination ; following the achievement of that object, the commander was directed to proceed in making discoveries through the wide extent of the Great Southern Ocean.

On August 26th,1768, the *Endeavour* sailed with a fair wind. The first port of call was Madeira to take on wine. The next port was Rio de Janeiro to obtain provisions. The governor, who appears to have been an ignorant man, did not treat the dignitaries with any civility, indeed the *Endeavour* was fired upon from the forts at Santa Cruz, when after three weeks she left the harbour.

Sailing down the coast of South America in December to the Falklands, the crew complained of the cold. They were then issued with jackets and trousers made of thick woollen material called 'Fearnought.' They next sailed from the Straits la Maire between Helen Island and Terra del Fuego. On anchoring in the Bay of Good Success several of the party went on shore. Thirty or forty natives soon appeared, but quickly fell back at a distance. Mr Banks and Dr Solander went forward, when two natives came towards them and sat down. As the explorers came nearer, the natives rose and threw away a stick which each had in their hands. This was taken as a sign of peace and a friendly relationship was established, some of the natives going on board the ship ; one of whom, it was supposed was a priest, who shouted all the time.

It being the middle of summer in those climes, Mr Banks, Dr Solander, Mr Green and Mr Monkhouse, with attendants, set out to visit a distant mountain. It was fine when they started out, but after they had negotiated a swamp, the weather quickly deteriorated, the cold being intense and snow falling heavily. Dr Solander warned his companions not to give way to sleep, but he was one of the first to feel tired and suggested they lay down. Mr Banks, not without the greatest difficulty, urged him on, but two black servants lay down and were frozen to death, and a seaman who remained with them almost shared the same fate. Out of provisions, they shared a night of great anxiety, their only food being a vulture which they had shot. They were glad when they returned to the ship and once refreshed set out again to inspect the land. The explorers found a tribe of about fifty persons, living in a 'village' of conical huts, roughly made of boughs, and open at the lee side. The people were stout, with painted faces and scantily covered with seal skins. Their diet consisted chiefly of shell fish.

Towards the end of January 1769, and in about three weeks the *Endeavour* got round the Cape Horn without ever once being brought under her close reefed topsails. There was a lack of wind and they arrived at George Island [Tahiti] on April 13th, having discovered en route several small islands, which Cook described as 'of no great note.'

As the ship approached the harbour, several canoes came off to meet her, their crews carrying green branches as a sign of friendship. The natives gladly traded their coconuts, apple-like fruit, bread fruit, and small fish in exchange for beads and other trifles. They also had a pig, but insisted on having a hatchet for it. Cook would not allow that for it would have set a precedent for the price of a pig.

The first person taken on board was Owhau, well-known to Mr Green and others who had been before with Captain Wallis. It was felt that Owhau would be useful to them, so he was warmly received.

Cook, a strict disciplinarian, issued a set of rules to govern the ships company in their dealings with the natives. They were as follows :

1. To endeavour by every fair means to cultivate a friendship with the natives; and to treat them with all humanity.

2. A proper person or persons will be appointed to trade with the natives for all manner of provisions, fruit and other productions of the earth ; and no officer or seaman, or other person belonging to the ship, except such as are so appointed, shall trade or offer to trade for any sort of provisions, fruit or other productions of the earth, unless they have leave to do so.

3. Every person employed on shore, on any duty whatsoever, is strictly to attend to the same ; and if by any neglect he loses any of his arms or working tools, or suffers them to be stolen, the full value thereof will be charged against his pay, according to the custom of the Navy in such cases ; and he shall receive such other punishment as the nature of the case may deserve.

4. The same penalty will be inflicted on every person who is found to embezzle, trade, or offer to trade with any part of the ships stores of what nature soever.

5. No sort of iron, or anything that is made of iron, or any sort of cloth, or

BAY OF FUNCHAL, MADERIA.

COOK'S ARRIVAL AT TAHITI.

other useful or necessary articles are to be given in exchange for anything but provisions.

On landing on shore, Cook was approached by the natives with great deference and presented with a green bough as an emblem of peace. The next day two natives of greater consequence than any that had yet appeared came off, called Matahah and Tootalah ; the former fixing on Mr Banks as his friend, and the latter on Cook. The ceremony consisted of the natives taking off a great part of their clothing and putting on that of their white friends. Cook, Mr Banks and others went on shore with these two chiefs and met another chief called Tabourai Tamaide, who invited them to his home, where he gave them a feast of fish, bread-fruit, coconuts and plantains. During the course of this repast Dr Solander and Mr Monkhouse discovered that their pockets had been picked. An opera glass and a snuff box were missing. Mr Banks struck the butt end of his musket violently on the ground at which most of the natives fled. The chief offered native cloth as compensation, but Mr Banks refused it, whereon the chief went out and in half an hour returned with the snuff box and the opera glass case, which was, to the consternation of the chief, empty. Leading Mr Banks by the hand, the chief rapidly conducted him to the house of a woman who on receiving some cloth and beads, went out and in half an hour returned with the opera glass.

A place was chosen from which to make the astronomical observation of the transit of Venus. A tent was set up and leaving a midshipman and a party of marines to guard it, Mr Banks and some of the gentlemen set off to obtain some livestock, with Owhau. Mr Banks killed three ducks with one shot. Shortly after this two shots were heard from the direction of the tent. On hurrying back there, it was discovered that a native had been killed. It seems that a native had suddenly seized a sentry's musket and the midshipman had ordered the marine to fire. Cook explained to the natives that though the English would allow no liberties to be taken, yet their desire was to treat them with kindness.

Mr Buchan, one of the landscape artists brought out by Mr Banks, suffered from fits and unfortunately died.

By April 26th, a fort had been completed and six swivel guns were mounted in it. Some of the chiefs visited the fort, including Tubourai Tamaide, whose wife on one occasion was threatened with death by the ships butcher, who coveted a stone which she had in her hand.

Having breached the rules laid down by Cook, the butcher was sentenced to be publicly flogged ; a standard punishment in the navy at that time, when the offender was stripped to the waist and tied to the mast and struck with the 'cat o' nine tails.' The native chiefs, having witnessed the first strokes, begged Cook to cease the punishment, but he would not allow it, at which the chiefs burst into tears.

About the beginning of May the quadrant vital to the purpose of the expedition was missing from the middle of the fort. Search was made among the natives and finally all the parts were retrieved. Observations were taken from two positions, one to the east, the other westwards. The weather being clear, the transit of Venus over the suns disc was observed with great advantage.

Captain Wallis had encountered a queen on the island and Cook was interested to meet her, but it was not until after the observations had been carried out that he was able to do so. She was called Oberea and presents were given to her. She had a priest called Tupia who expressed a strong desire to accompany Cook on his further voyages after leaving Tahiti.

As Mr Banks was sitting in his boat trading with the natives, some women who were strangers advanced in procession towards him. The rest of the natives on each side of him gave way, forming a lane for the women to pass, who, coming up to Mr Banks, presented him with some parrot feathers, and various kinds of plants. Tupia, who stood by Mr Banks, acted as master of ceremonies, and receiving the branches, which were brought at six different times, laid them down in the boat, After this some large pieces of cloth were brought, consisting of nine pieces, which being divided into three parcels, one of the women called Oorattooa, who appeared to be the principal, stepping up on one of them, lifted up her clothes, and then, with an unaffected air of innocence and simplicity, turned round three times. This ceremony was repeated with similar circumstances, on the other parcels of cloth ; and the whole being presented to Mr Banks, the women saluted him ; in return for such extraordinary favours he made them such present as he thought would be acceptable. This ceremony at first may have the appearance of indecency to European eyes at that time, but when it was observed that it was a stated custom, it must have tended, in some degree, to obviate all censure.

In the evening the officers of the fort were visited by Oberea, and Otheorea. her favourite female attendant, who was a very agreeable girl, and whom they were more pleased to see, because it had been reported that she was either sick or dead.

Tupia had been a minister of Oberea at the height of her power, now considerably diminished. He had formed a particular attachment to the English that visited the island in the *Dolphin,* under the command of Captain Wallis. He was also the chief Tahowa, or priest of the island and consequently well acquainted with the religion of his country as well as its ceremonies and principals, to which he had added a knowledge of navigation, and an acquaintance of the number and situation of the neighbouring islands.

Before leaving the island Mr Banks planted a quantity of seeds of watermelon, oranges, lemons, limes and other plants and trees which he had collected at Rio de Janeiro. On July 13th, 1769, the *Endeavour* left Tahiti to try and find the supposed Southern Continent. Tupia had informed Cook that four islands, which he called Huaheine, Ulietea, Otaha, and Bolabola were about one to two days sail off Tahiti and that an abundance of provisions could be obtained there. Due to a light wind it was three days before they reached Huaheine. When the *Endeavour* drew in towards the island, many canoes came out to meet her, but remained at a distance until they saw Tupia, who was able to converse with them. Oree, the king of the island and his wife were in one of the canoes. On being assured that they would be treated as friends, they came on board the ship. As a mark of friendship the king asked to exchange names, he becoming King Cookee and Cook became Captain Oree. On landing the explorers were treated to a feast in which certain religious rituals were practised, Tupia taking the role of a priest. Next day some trading took place, some pigs were exchanged for axes, and with some medals presented to the king, the adventurers took their leave.

Ulietea was the next island visited, where, within the coral reef they found a good harbour. As the *Endeavour* anchored two canoes came off, each bringing a pig and a woman. The pigs were presented as a gift and the women were given some trinkets in return..

Cook took possession of the island, hoisting the Union Jack in the name of King George III. Mr Banks visited a long house in which he saw the model of a canoe, about a yard in length, which had some human jaw bones attached to it. Tupia affirmed that they were those of natives of the island. The harbour was called Oopoa and bad weather prevented the *Endeavour*

HUAHEINE, SOCIETY ISLANDS.

PORTRAIT OF CAPTAIN COOK.
About 1771.

from leaving it for two days. The ship received a scrape from the coral and it was later discovered that there was a leak. Cook returned to Ulietea and put into a harbour on the opposite side of the island to take in ballast and water.

It appeared that the island had been recently conquered by the subjects of Opoony, king of Bolabola, whom Cook desired to meet. Instead of seeing a fine-looking warrior, he found a withered, decrepit wretch, half blind with age, and yet he was the terror of all the surrounding islands.

Being a sailor, Cook was naturally interested in the boats which the natives used and particularly in their construction. The canoes were often large, and constructed with great labour and ingenuity. they were of two builds ; one, the Icaha, for short excursions, was wall-sided, with a flat bottom ; the other, the Pahie, for longer voyages, was bow-sided, with a sharp bottom. The fighting Ivaha was the largest ; the head and stern were raised sometimes seventeen feet or more above the sides, which were only three feet out of the water. These vessels took the form of a catamaran, the two hulls being joined together by poles about three feet apart. Towards the head a platform was raised, about twelve feet long, wider than the boats, and on this platform stood the fighting men, armed with slings and spears ; for bows and arrows were only used in sports. The rowers sat below the platform. Some of the pahies were often sixty feet long.

The adventurers were able to able to obtain a good supply of hogs, poultry and other provisions. Unfortunately the livestock were unaccustomed to European grain and consequently died.

To the six islands which had been visited or seen, namely, Ulietea, Otaha, Bolabola, Huaheine, Tubal, and Maurna, Cook gave the name of the Society Islands. Tahiti was not included in the group, but continued to be known as King George's Island.

THE SEARCH FOR A SOUTHERN CONTINENT

ON AUGUST 9th, the *Endeavour* left Ulietea and began to search for the supposed Southern Continent in earnest. On the 13th an island which Tupia called Oheteroa, was sighted, when Mr Gore took the ships boat, accompanied by Mr Banks, Dr Solander and Tupia, to attempt a landing. At the sight of the boat a number of natives appeared, armed with long lances. Two men swam out towards the boat, but could not keep up with it. Another native reached the boat, but Mr Gore refused to let him be taken in despite the pleas of Mr Banks, who was hoping to establish a good relationship with the islanders. On attempting to land, Mr Gore was met by several natives coming off in a canoe and they attempted to capture the boat. They soon fled when muskets were fired above their heads as a warning. No harbour or suitable landing place could be found and the islanders being everywhere hostile, the attempt to land was abandoned, and the *Endeavour* was turned south two days later.

On August 25th, the explorers celebrated the anniversary of the setting out from England. A Cheshire cheese was cut and a cask of porter was uncorked. On the south a comet was seen and a heavy sea and a strong gale followed. During the whole of September Cook continued his course to the westward. Quite a few seals were seen asleep on the surface of the sea and various birds were perceived and this was taken as an indication of the ship approaching land. On October 6th the look-out on the mast head sighted land, bearing west by north. By evening it was visible from the deck, although it was the evening of the following day before the voyagers were near enough to observe it more clearly. It appeared to be of great expanse, with four or five ranges of hills, beyond which was a chain of mountains. They believed they had found the *Terra Australis Incognita*. A bay was seen, with smoke rising from the shore and it was resolved that a landing would be postponed until morning The following afternoon the *Endeavour* was brought to anchor in a bay off the mouth of a river.

Cook, Mr Banks and Dr Solander, with a party of men in the yawl and pinnace, landed on the east side of the river, but seeing some natives on the west side, the yawl crossed over, the gentlemen landed, leaving the yawl in the charge of four boys. On the gentlemen landing, the natives ran away. The explorers approached some huts and when they were some distance from the yawl, four warriors with long lances rushed out of a wood and made for the yawl. The men in the pinnace called to the boys to row down the stream. The firing of muskets failed to stop the attackers until one of the natives, taking aim at the boys with his spear, when the coxswain of the pinnace shot him dead. The other three tried to drag the fallen man away, but soon took flight. Cook and his companions examined the body of the warrior, who had been shot through the heart. He was of middle height, with a light complexion. One side of his face was tattooed in spiral regular lines, and his hair was tied in a knot at the top of his head. He wore a garment of fine cloth such as the visitors had not seen before.

Next day a further landing was made and the marines were sent for in case of trouble. The natives made it clear that the voyagers should depart. Tupia, who they could understand, told them that the visitors wanted to trade for provisions. They said they would trade if the English would cross the river to them. Cook said he was willing to do so if they would put aside their arms. This they refused to do ; Tupia warning the captain that the natives were hostile ; but Cook invited the islanders to come across to him. One man stripped and swam across unarmed. He was later followed by about twenty others, some of whom were armed. They tried to snatch the visitors weapons and Tupia warned them that they would be killed. One of them grabbed Mr Green's hanger. Mr Banks fired at him, but he continued to wave the hanger about, whereupon Mr Monkhouse shot him and he dropped. The natives seeing this, began to attack and more shots were fired and several of their fellows being wounded, they retreated up river.

Captain Cook was dismayed that blood had been shed and gave the name of Poverty Bay to that place. In reality the country where they met such an unfriendly reception was New Zealand. Next day the *Endeavour* began to sail from the bay, but became becalmed, whereon several canoes came off to her and fifty of the natives were persuaded to come on board. Presents were made by the ships officers and the natives gave all they had in return, even their canoe paddles. The next day an old chief came off in a canoe, but he would not board the *Endeavour,* until Tupia assured him that the strangers did not eat men. This remark prompted the Englishmen to suspect that the natives practised cannibalism.

The women of New Zealand, however, had proved irresistible to the sailors, and even the officers ; understandable when such lengthy periods had been spent at sea. Prostitution was also practised, the women granting their favours for small trinkets. Needless to say, Captain Cook did not indulge in these sexual activities.

The point of land made to the north of Poverty Bay proved to be the most easterly point of New Zealand and was called East Cape. Cook now turned south when an island close to the mainland was passed. Some natives came off in canoes, but appeared to be hostile. The ship being dangerously close to a reef, soundings were being made when five large canoes, filled with armed warriors came off. Muskets were fired over their heads, but they took no notice, so a four-pounder, loaded with grape shot, though fired wide, put them to flight. It was the policy to fire above the attackers heads to frighten them, only to kill them when all else had failed. Next day as the *Endeavour* sailed further along the coast, a war party in five large canoes came off in a threatening attitude. A wide shot from the four-pounder soon made them retreat.

Cook was getting desperate for supplies by now, so when the next day found the ship further along the coast, he was pleased to trade with some natives, although they only had stale fish to sell. One of the natives stole a coat. Tupia's boy, Tayeto, was one of those leaning over the side of the ship to hand up articles, when he was abducted by some of the natives and put in their canoe. On orders the marines fired at the canoe, killing one of the abductors. Tayeto dived over the side of the canoe and swam back to the ship. Cook named the headland off which this drama took place as Cape Kidnappers.

On tacking and standing to the north-west, the ship was off a bluff headland with yellowish cliffs, when some canoes containing some native chiefs came off and made friendly gestures, inviting the strangers to come on shore. This was not possible until the evening, when they were met by small groups. Cook decided to obtain fresh water and the operation went ahead the next day. While at the watering place, the natives performed some war songs, the women contorting their faces, rolling their eyes and sticking out their tongues. The reader may have observed Maories performing in such a manner at rugby matches, or on ceremonial occasions, such as a Royal visit. This bay was called by the natives Tolaga. Wood and water and an abundance of wild celery, which proved an effective antiscorbutic, being got on board, the anchor was weighed and the *Endeavour* headed north again.

New Zealand was first visited by Tasman in 1642, but he did not land there. Cook described the natives as 'being rather above the common size, they are a very dark brown colour with long black hair. The men often go naked with only a narrow belt about their waists ; the women on the contrary never appear naked.'

In order to observe the transit of Mercury, a large inlet was entered and the natives at first appeared in a hostile manner. When Tupia explained to them that the English had superior weapons, the islanders started to trade, a large number of mackerel being obtained, the sailors salting enough for a months supply. A fine day allowed Cook and Mr Green to make a satisfactory observation of Mercury, and the name of 'Mercury Bay' was given to the location.

As the *Endeavour* proceeded along the coast, several attempts at thieving were made by the natives, but gradually a friendly relationship was established. On leaving the Bay of Islands, the ship grazed a rock to the windward of her with great violence, but it seemed that no damage was sustained.

Cook discovered that New Zealand consisted of two islands and he spent six months circumnavigating both of them. The *Endeavour* left New Zealand on April 1st,1770 steering towards New Holland ; all of the east point part of which remained undiscovered. Nine days afterwards a tropical bird was seen, but a sounding could not find the seabed. At 6 a.m. on April 19th, Mr Hicks, the first lieutenant, sighted land. Cook gave the name of New South Wales to this northern extremity of Australia. Strong winds kept the *Endeavour* from the shore, but at last a sheltered bay was discovered. The pinnace was sent ashore to take soundings and the ship beat into the bay and anchored two miles within it in six fathoms of water. Some natives were seen with painted bodies and brandishing long spears. All of the aborigines were naked and most of them ignored the strangers. Two men with spears made threatening gestures and Cook tried to parley with them, but it took some musket fire to make them run off. Fresh water was found and Mr Banks and Dr Solander discovered an abundance of plants, so the name of Botany Bay was given to the area.

During the *Endeavours* stay in Botany Bay, Captain Cook had the Union Jack hoisted every day on shore, and had the ships name and the date of her visit carved on a tree near the watering place.

They sailed from Botany Bay on May 6th and while speeding on her course one beautiful moonlight night, the ship struck a reef, and instantly all on board were awake with the fearsome prospect of a shipwreck on an inhospitable coast. All heavy objects were thrown overboard to help keep the ship afloat. A temporary repair was made by drawing a sail over the leak. This emergency repair enabled the ship to reach an inlet which they called 'Endeavour River'; [now known as Cooktown] and the ship was beached there for forty-nine days while repairs were made, the vessel being tied to an iron-wood tree. Besides the leak, which was on the starboard side, the ship had suffered extensive damage on the larboard. The sheathing from the bow on that side having been torn off and a great part of the false keel was gone. The carpenters immediately began their work and a forge was set up for the blacksmiths to make bolts and nails.

Captain Cook saw a kangaroo for the first time, while Mr Banks was shooting pigeons and crows to provide fresh flesh, for some of the crew, including Tupia and Mr Green, were suffering from scurvy. Fish were caught and Mr Banks found some kale, which served as greens. Mr Banks shot a kangaroo and it was dressed for dinner, being greatly enjoyed. Besides kangaroos, dingoes were seen, which our explorers called wild dogs which they considered partly resembled foxes and wolves. Some turtles were also captured and a visiting party of aborigines tried to steal one. Followed on shore by Mr Banks, one of them seized a brand from under the pitch-kettle, and whirling it round set fire to some dry grass. The fire rapidly spread, destroying the woodwork of the smiths' forge. It caught a sow and some piglets, scorching them to death. The fire spread into the woods ; the natives attempting to cause further conflagration, a gun with some small shot was fired, followed by a bullet near them, which put them to flight. Later they returned led by an old man with a pointless spear. Mr Banks went forward to meet him and on returning the natives' spears, which they had abandoned, friendly relations were established.

At length the ship was ready for sea again, but the prospect of getting out into the open sea was precarious, to say the least, by the coral reef - the Great Barrier Reef - which hemmed in the *Endeavour*. Heavy gales delayed their departure until August 4th. It took all the skill of the seamen to negotiate the labyrinth of coral rock. At night a gale blew up and the ship began to drive. All the appliances of seamanship were put into operation, but still she drove, when the top gallant masts were got down, and yards and topmasts struck, she then rode securely. The *Endeavour* continued in this position until the 10th, when Cook resolved to search for a passage close in shore to the northward, she got underway and stood in that direction with the boats exploring ahead. Hour after hour was spent searching for a passage and at length one was found. The seas which the ship now encountered widened the leaks and they admitted nine inches of water an hour. The ship was later threatened by being driven onto another reef, so great that it stretched as far as the eye could see. The sea was too deep to anchor so the only prospect open to them was rowing. The pinnace was under repair and useless, so the long boat and the yawls were set ahead to tow, and sweeps were got out. The carpenters worked furiously to repair the pinnace. They battled to keep the ship off the reef, but eventually Mr

COOK CLAIMS AUSTRALIA FOR KING GEORGE III.

Hicks discovered a passage through which the ship safely passed and anchored in nineteen-fathom water.

Captain Cook now resolved to keep close to land for fear of missing the passage between Australia and New Guinea. The passage was found, but before leaving the east coast of Australia, which Cook was convinced no other European had seen, he landed on an island, which he called Possession Island, and raised the Union flag, claiming the country in the name of King George III. Three volleys of small arms were fired and answered from the ship. Ten natives were seen on the island, who seemed astounded at this ceremony, which took place on August 21st, 1770. Point Hicks, where they had first sighted Australia is now called Cape Everard.

A course was set for New Guinea where only one landing was made on September 3rd. The landing party were threatened by some natives and fired some small shot. Cook had no intention, he said, of invading the island and thought it best to return to the ship. En route to Batavia they called at an island partly under the Dutch East India Company, where they received some welcome refreshments.

On passing through Straits of Sunda, the *Endeavour* was boarded by the Dutch authorities and enquiries were made as to the object of the voyage. Captain Cook was received into port by the Dutch governor with courtesy and kindness. It was nearly ten weeks before the repairs to the ship were completed. In one place the planking was so worn by the grinding of the rocks, that it did not exceed the thickness of a man's shoe sole. Her frame in many places was much shattered, and her pumps had become rotten and useless.

The climate did not suit our travellers and within a few days many fell ill. Tupia was seriously incapacitated, as were Dr Solander and Mr Banks. Mr Monkhouse, the ships surgeon was the first to die. Tayeto, Tupia's boy, whom he loved like a son, died and his death hastened Tupia's own demise.

On December 26th, 1770 the *Endeavour* set sail with a light breeze. By now she was something of a hospital ship and on the passage to the Cape of Good Hope, thirty people had died. Reaching Table Bay on March 15th, the ship was anchored and the sick were taken ashore, where many recovered, the Cape Town climate being healthy.

By May 23rd the rigging and sails of the *Endeavour* had deteriorated so much that every day something was giving way, but on July 10th the Lizard Point was sighted by Nicholas Young, who had first descried New Zealand.

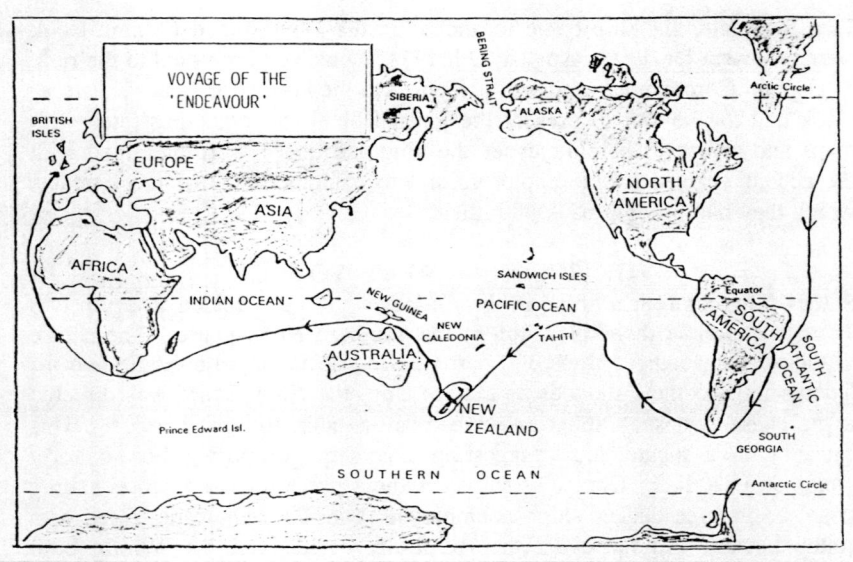

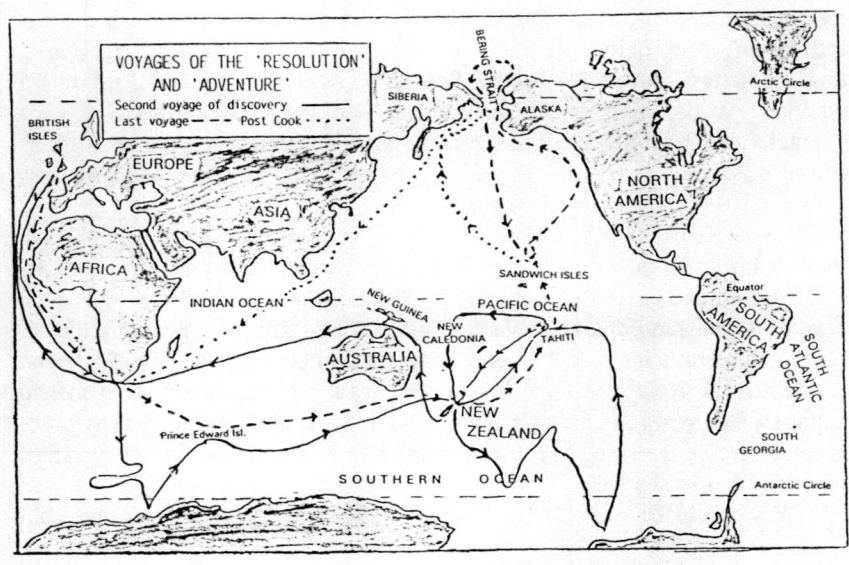

Two days later the ship came to anchor in the Downs, and Captain Cook went ashore at Deal. On August 29th, 1771, Cook was promoted to the rank of Captain Commander, and was presented to the king at St.James's Palace. Cook had the honour to present the journal of his voyage, illustrated with maps and charts. Their majesties the king and queen were delighted with the accounts given by the explorers and to examine some of the artefacts which they had brought back with them.

THE SECOND GREAT VOYAGE

SOON after his return home in the *Endeavour* it was decided to equip two ships to complete the exploration of the Southern Hemisphere. The nature of the voyage required ships of a particular construction, and the *Endeavour* having gone to the Falklands as a store ship, the Navy-Board was directed to purchase two such ships as were most suitable for this service. This caused quite a debate, some suggesting large ships, proposing those of forty guns, or East India Company ships. Others preferred large good sailing frigates, or three-decked ships as employed in the Jamaica trade, fitted with round houses. In the event the Admiralty decided on two Whitby-built colliers. The *Drake,* of 462 tons, and the *Raleigh,* of 336 tons were purchased from Captain William Hammond of Hull which were employed by him in the coal trade. The ships were about fourteen or sixteen months old, having been built by Fishburns. The former was renamed *Resolution* and the latter, *Adventure.* The *Resolution* was sent to Deptford to be equipped, while the *Adventure* was sent to Woolwich to be refitted.

James Cook was appointed to the command of the *Resolution ;* and Tobias Furneaux (who had been second lieutenant with Captain Wallis), was promoted to command the *Adventure.*

While the ships were being made ready, Cook requested three weeks leave to visit his aged father in Yorkshire. This was granted and in December 1771 he made the journey to Great Ayton to see his father, now aged seventy-seven, and doubtless visited his mother's grave in the churchyard. During his stay, he rode horseback over the moors to see his old friend Captain John Walker. Mary Proud, the Walker's house-keeper, who had supplied the young James with candles while he studied in the Whitby attic, greeted him by throwing her arms around him and crying, 'Oh honey James how glad I is to see thee !'

Mr Banks and Dr Solander had intended going on the second voyage, but not finding the accommodation on board which they considered necessary for the comfort and convenience of themselves and their servants, they gave up the project. According to James Boswell, even Dr Samuel Johnson thought of going, though he speedily abandoned the idea. Two astronomers, William Wales and William Bayley, were engaged by the Board of Longitude, the former sailing in the *Resolution,* the latter in the *Adventure.* William Hodges and John Reinhold Forster, together with his son were appointed by the Admiralty, the former as landscape artist, the latter two as natural history observers.

Captain Cook's first lieutenant was Robert P.Cooper, his second Charles Clerke, who had accompanied him on his first great voyage, as had the third lieutenant, Richard Pickersgill. Joseph Gilbert was master. Two of the warrant officers and several of the petty officers had also been with him on his first voyage and he declared himself 'to be perfectly satisfied with the choice of officers.' John Edgecombe was the marines officer-in-command. Captain Furneaux had Joseph Shank as his first lieutenant and Arthur Kempe as second. His master was Peter Fannin. James Scott was the marine commander. The ships company of the *Resolution* totalled 112, with 81 in the *Adventure.*

Following the experience of the many cases of scurvy suffered on his former expedition, Captain Cook took especial care with the diet of his sailors, making alterations to the usual fare provided by the Navy and Victualling Boards. When completed each ship had two-and-a-half years provisions on board. Malt was used to make sweet wort ; Sour-kraut, a wholesome vegetable food which keeps well and is a great antiscorbutic ; salted cabbage ; portable broth ; marmalade of carrots were just some of the foods used. Beer could be produced from inspissated juice of wort.

The frame of a small vessel of twenty tons burden was properly prepared and put on board each of the ships, to be set up to serve as tenders in any emergency, or to transport the crew in case the ship was lost. Fishing nets, lines and hooks were provided to enable fish to be caught. Merchandise was provided for the purpose of trading with the natives who had no use for money.

The *Resolution* sailed from Deptford, April 9th,1772, but was detained at Woolwich by easterly winds until the 22nd, when the ships fell down Long Reach, being joined the next day by the *Adventure.* Here both ships received on board their powder, guns, gunners' stores and the marines. On

May 10th they left Long Reach with orders to call at Plymouth ; but in plying down the river, the *Resolution* was found to be very crank, [meaning the rigging was too weighty for the hull], which made it necessary to put into Sheerness, in order to remove the cause by making some alterations to her upper works.. Modifications were complete by June 22nd and on July 3rd the ship joined with the *Adventure* in Plymouth Sound.

Captain Cook received his orders dated June 25th, directing him to take command of the *Adventure* and make his way to Madeira to take on wine, and then to proceed to the Cape of Good Hope, where he was to refresh the ships companies and take on provisions as required. After leaving the Cape of Good Hope, he was to proceed to the southward, and endeavour to fall in with Cape Circumcision. If he discovered this cape, he had to satisfy himself whether it was part of a continent, or part of an island. If it was the former he had to explore it and make observations of every kind which might be useful to other navigators or commerce. He was to continue in this service, and making discoveries, either to the eastward or westward, keeping in as high a latitude as he could, and prosecuting his discoveries as near the South Pole as possible, so long as the conditions of the ships, the health of their crews, and the state of their provisions would admit of ; taking care to reserve as much of the latter as would enable him to reach some known port, where he was to procure a sufficiency to bring him home to England. But if the cape turned out to be an island only, or if he was unable to find the cape, he was in the first place to make a survey and then stand to the southward and continue to circle the globe, after which he was to proceed to the Cape of Good Hope and from there to Spithead. If the *Resolution* was lost, the voyage was to continue in the *Adventure*. A copy of these orders was given by Cook to Captain Furneaux and they agreed that if they became separated, Madeira was appointed for the first place of rendezvous.

At six o'clock in the morning of July 13th the second great voyage began as the *Resolution,* in company with the *Adventure,* sailed from Plymouth Sound. Sixteen days later, in the evening, Cook anchored his ship in Funchiale Road, Madeira. Next morning he fired a salute of eleven guns to the garrison, which compliment was immediately returned. Going on shore with Captain Furneaux, the two Forsters and Mr Wales, they were received by a Mr Sills from the vice-consul, who conducted them to the house of Loughmans, the most important English merchant in the town. This gentleman not only obtained leave for Mr Forster to search the island for plants, but procured them every other thing they wanted.

Having taken on board water. wine and other necessities, they left Madeira on August 1st, steering southwards with a fine gale at north-east. On the 4th they passed Palma, one of the Canary Islands. The next day, sighting the Isle of Ferro, passing it at a distance of fourteen leagues.

Some of the water had been used to make beer and Cook realised there would be insufficient to reach the Cape of Good Hope without rationing it. He resolved to stop at St.Jago for a supply. Bearing south-west they passed the island of Bonavista, and on the 10th, passing the island of Mayo they anchored in Port Praya, in the island of St.Jago. An officer was at once despatched to ask leave to obtain water and buy refreshments, which was granted. Having obtained water, hogs, goats, fowls and fruit ; they were underway again on the 14th.

An unfortunate incident occurred shortly after leaving St.Jago. A carpenter who was over the side, fitting one of the scuttles, fell into the sea. he was not noticed until he went down under the stern of the *Resolution,* and the crew were unable to save him. His loss was greatly mourned for he was a sober man and a skilled workman.

Heavy rain was experienced followed by a dead calm which lasted for twenty-four hours. Cook spoke with Captain Furneaux who reported that one of his officers had died. None of Cook's crew were sick, but he regarded heavy rain as a great promoter of sickness in a hot climate. To prevent this he took every necessary precaution by airing and drying the ship with fires between the decks, and getting the crew to air their bedding, and to wash and dry their clothes.

On September 8th, the line of longtitude of eight degrees west was passed and the usual ceremonies of ducking etc., were practised. On the 27th a sail was sighted to the west. Cook could not make out from colours she was flying whether it was Portuguese or St.George's ensign, as it was at some distance. He did not wish to get closer, or to speak to her. Variable weather slowed their progress. On October 11th they observed an eclipse of the moon.

On the 29th the Cape of Good Hope was reached ; spending the night standing off, the crew witnessed the whole sea being illuminated, or, what the seamen called, on fire. Mr Banks and Dr Solander had previously told Cook that it was caused by sea insects. Mr Forster seemed not to share that opinion, so Cook had some buckets of water drawn up from alongside the ship, which were found to be full of an innumerable quantity of small globular insects, about the size of a pin head, and quite transparent.

As soon as the ships were anchored they were visited by the Captain of the port, some officers, a doctor and Mr Brandt, at whose house they would be set up. The purpose of boarding the ships was to take an account of the ships ; to enquire into the health of the crews ; and in particular, if the small-pox was on board ; a thing they dreaded above all others at the Cape.

Baron Plettenberg, the governor, received Cook, Captain Furneaux and the two Forsters with great civility and promised to help them procure anything they needed. He told them that two French ships came from the Mauritius about eight months ago, having discovered land, in the latitude of forty-eight degrees south. They had sailed some forty miles of the island when they were driven off by a severe gale, losing some of their boats and people. The captain of *La Fortune* had been sent home to France with details of their discovery. The governor also informed them that in March last two other French ships had touched at the Cape on their way to the South Pacific Ocean, where they intended to make discoveries.

The English officers fixed lodgings at Mr Brandt's house and he helped them to obtain provisions, while the seamen on board were engaged in overhauling the rigging ; and the carpenters in caulking the ships sides and decks etc. Messrs Wales and Bayley took their instruments on shore, in order to make astronomical observations to check the accuracy of Mr Kendal's watch, which proved its precision.

A few days later, two Dutch Indiamen arrived from Holland, after a passage of four months. One ship had lost one hundred-and-fifty men ; and the other forty-one through the scurvy and other fatal diseases. The Dutch at the Cape, finding their hospital inadequate for so large a number of admissions as were required, immediately laid the foundations for a new and larger one.

It was November 18th by the time all the stores were aboard the ships. Mr Joseph Shank, the first lieutenant of the *Adventure,* having been taken ill, applied to Cook for leave to quit and return home. Cook consented and appointed Arthur Kemp in his place, with Mr Burney, one of Cook's midshipmen, as second lieutenant. Mr Forster met a Swedish gentleman who had studied under Dr Linnaeus. Forster persuaded Cook to allow him to join the expedition.

At three o'clock in the afternoon of November 22nd, the two British ships left the Cape to go in search of a Southern Continent. Once clear of land, Cook directed the course for Cape Circumcision. Two days later they saw many albatrosses, some of which were caught and cooked with some fresh mutton and were much relished by the sailors. Anticipating that they would soon be experiencing some cold weather, Captain Cook ordered that each man be given the Fearnought jacket and trousers allowed them by the Admiralty. He also instructed that slops to be served to such as were in want. On the 29th they ran into a storm, which continued, with a few intervals of moderate weather, until December 6th. This gale, attended with rain and hail, blew with such violence at times that they were unable to carry any sails. They were blown far to the eastward of their intended course, and no hopes were left of reaching Cape Circumcision. The greatest tragedy, however, was the loss of livestock, consisting of sheep, hogs and geese. Indeed, the sudden transition from warm mild weather to extreme cold and wet, made every man in the ships feel its effect. Some extra spirit was given over and above the allowance to which each man was entitled.

At eight o'clock in the morning of the 8th, two penguins were seen and some sea or rock weed. Soundings were taken without finding ground at one hundred fathoms. The wind blew in squalls, with snow showers, but moderated by eight o'clock in the evening, when Captain Cook signalled to Captain Furneaux to make sail, and soon after the *Resolution* made sail as well, but later in the evening they had to take in the top-sails and main-sail, and brought too, under fore-sail and mizzen. The wind at north-west blew a fresh gale, accompanied with a very high sea. During the night there was a sharp frost with snow.

In the morning of the 10th sail was made under courses and top-sails close reefed. Cook made signal to the *Adventure*, to make sail and lead. At eight o'clock they saw an 'island of ice' [an iceberg] to their westward. Soon after the wind moderated, and they let all the reefs out of the top-sails, got the spritsail-yard out, and top-gallant mast up. The weather became hazy and Cook called the *Adventure*, by signal under his stern ; which was no sooner done, than the haze increased so much, with snow and sleet, that they did not see an iceberg, which they were steering directly for, till they were less than a mile from it. Cook judged it to be about fifty feet high, and half a mile in circumference. It was flat on top, and its sides rose in a perpendicular direction, against which the sea broke exceedingly high. Captain Furneaux at first took this ice for land, and hauled off from it, until called back by signal. It was necessary to proceed with caution so they reefed their top-sails, and sounded, but found no ground with one hundred and fifty fathoms.

At daylight in the morning of the 13th, they made sail southwards with the wind at west, having a fresh gale with sleet and snow. Some birds about the size of pigeons, with blackish bills and feet were seen. Cook said he had never seen such birds before, and Mr Forster had no knowledge of them. They then passed between two icebergs, which lay a little distance from each other. On the 12th they still experienced thick hazy weather, with sleet and snow ; in that they had to proceed with caution on account of the icebergs ; six of which were passed that day ; some of them about two miles in circumference and sixty feet high. Such was the force of the sea that it broke right over them. Captain Cook said that 'for a few moments the sight was pleasing to the eye ; but when one reflected on the danger, the mind was filled with horror ; for, were a ship to get against the weather side of one of these islands when the sea runs high, she would be dashed to pieces in a moment.' Penguins were seen as they kept on the southward.

At noon on the 13th, they were in the latitude of fifty-four degrees south, which is the latitude of Cape Circumcision, discovered in 1739 by M.Bouvet, but they were one hundred and eighteen leagues in that latitude. More and more icebergs were seen, but soundings at one hundred and fifty fathoms revealed no bottom. They bore away along the edge of the ice, steering south-south-east and south-east, according to the north side of it, where they saw many whales, penguins, some white birds, pintadoes, etc.

At eight o'clock Captain Cook sent on board for Captain Furneaux to fix a rendezvous in case of separation ; and some other matters for keeping together. Furneaux returned to his ship and they proceeded along the ice.

After they had travelled thirty leagues along the edge of the ice, experiencing many icebergs on the way, Cook decided to run thirty or forty leagues to the east, afterwards to try and get to the southwards. Dangerous as it is to sail among icebergs, Captain Cook believed it a far more serious prospect to be locked in an ice field. Two of his sailors had been in the Greenland whalers ; one of them in a ship that had lain for nine weeks, the other for six weeks, in that kind of ice, which they called packed ice. Cook was determined to see if there was any land beyond these ice fields, as was supposed. Continuous soundings were made but no bottom could be found. Mr Forster shot some penguins and other birds. It was a belief that penguins never go far from land, as they must go on shore to breed. Eighty-six penguins were counted on one iceberg, in the lee of which the ship was becalmed..

By early January 1773, Cook had reached the opinion that there was no land and changed the course for the south. They saw the moon for the first time since leaving the Cape of Good Hope, and took astronomical observations. On the 17th they crossed the Antarctic Circle. Clearer weather brought an improved range of vision and they counted thirty-eight icebergs and saw many whales playing about the ice. Passing near an iceberg they observed it falling to pieces, by the cracking noise it made, which was equal to the report of a four-pounder.

At times Captain Cook sent for Captain Furneaux to come aboard the *Resolution,* to discuss matters. At times he commanded the ships to separate by some four miles. On February 8th a thick fog descended and Cook fired guns every hour. A signal was made to the *Adventure,* but no reply was given. The commander feared a separation had taken place. He had instructed Captain Furneaux that in such an event to cruise for three days in the place they last saw each other. Cook therefore continued making short boards and firing half-hour guns until the afternoon of the 9th, at which time the weather cleared to give visibility for several leagues. There was no sign of the *Adventure.*

On February 16th the Aurora Australis was witnessed. Cook said he had never heard of the phenomenon being seen before. The 21st, in the morning, having little wind and a smooth sea, two favourable circumstances for taking up ice, from which to make drinking water, they steered for the largest iceberg ahead of them, which was reached by noon. Finding a good quantity of loose ice, Cook ordered out the boats. Whilst this was proceeding the iceberg, which was half-a-mile in circumference and three to four hundred feet high, turned nearly bottom up. Its height was neither increased or diminished by this happening. Happily the boats were safe from this dangerous circumstance. Although it was summer, Captain Cook and many of his crew suffered from chilblains in their toes and fingers.

LAND AT LAST

HAVING found no Southern Continent, Captain Cook decided to make for Van Dieman's Land, in order to satisfy himself it joined the coast of New South Wales. The wind, however, blew between the north and the west, which did not permit him to touch at that place, so he set a course for New Zealand, which was spotted from the mast head on March 25th, and at noon from the deck. They set full sail for the land, but before they could reach it, a thick fog descended, along with a heavy gale, obliging them to stand off overnight. The next morning they steered for Dusky Bay, on the West Cape. Eventually an anchorage was found in fifty fathoms of water, near enough to shore to reach it with a hawser. This was at three in the afternoon of March 26th, 1773, after having been at sea for one hundred and seventeen days, in which time they had sailed 3,660 leagues, without ever sighting land. Only one man suffered from the scurvy, justifying Cook's precautions and special diets.

Not entirely happy with their first anchorage, Cook sent Lieutenant Pickersgill over to the south-east side of the bay to search for a better. On his return the lieutenant reported that he had found a good harbour with every convenience. A boat was sent to catch fish and this proved to be a successful and beneficial exercise. Cook decided to stay some time in this locality, which he had only previously viewed from a distance, and no one had ever landed there before. The ship was steered into Pickersgill Harbour and was moored head and stern in a small creak, where fresh water was available. Wood for fuel and wildfowl for food were here in abundance. The ships yards were locked in the trees ; places were cleared in the woods to set up the astronomer's observatory and the forges to repair the ironwork; and coopers to repair the casks ; and the sail-makers to mend the sails.

The few sheep and goats which had survived the voyage in the Antarctic, were not in a very good state. They would not eat the coarse grass, or the foliage of bushes, and upon examination it was discovered that their teeth were loose.

On the 28th, some of the officers went up the bay in a small boat on a shooting party ; but discovering natives, they returned before noon to acquaint Captain Cook ; these being the first humans encountered so far. On searching himself, Cook found a canoe hauled up on the shore near two small huts. No person could be seen, so he concluded that they must have taken refuge in the woods. Some trinkets were left in the canoe. They could smell smoke, but Cook thought it best to search no further. It was not until April 6th, while returning from a shooting expedition, that natives were seen. Captain Cook was with the Forsters and Mr Hodges, when they were hallooed by a man who was standing on a rock, with a club in his hand. Behind him at the edge of a wood, stood two women, with spears in their hands. At first he showed fear at the approach of Cook, but did not move from the spot. The captain went up to him and embraced him, giving him gifts, which allayed his fears. The women joined in and a dialogue took place, each party not understanding the chit-chat. Next morning, Captain Cook, Mr Forster and Mr Hodges made a return visit to the natives, taking with them various gifts. They received the presents with great indifference, apart from the hatchets and spike-nails. The Englishmen now met the rest of the family which consisted of the man, his two wives (as was supposed) a young women, a boy of fourteen and three small children, the youngest of which was still at the breast. Their home, in the woods, consisted of two mean huts made from the bark of trees. Their canoe was a small double one, just large enough to transport the family from place to place. A week or so later the natives came down to the harbour, but could not be persuaded to go out to the ship, but sat on the shore talking to some of the sailors. It was noted that they only spoke to sailors that they had mistaken for women. To one man in particular, the young women showed an extraordinary fondness until she discovered his sex, after which she would not allow him to go near her. Whether it was that she before took him for one of her own sex ; or that the man had taken some liberties with her which she then resented, Captain Cook was unable to say. By evening the natives had taken up quarters about one hundred yards from the watering-place, which Cook took as a great mark of confidence. During some spells of rain the natives returned to their huts. By April 17th they returned to the moorage and the chief and his daughter were induced to go on board the ship. Before doing so, the man took a small green branch and struck the ships side several times, repeating a speech or prayer. This custom and manner of making friends was practised by all the natives in the South Seas that Cook encountered.

Another tribe of natives was discovered during one of the duck-shooting parties and Cook established a friendly relationship with one man.

By the end of April the *Resolution* was ready for sea again, but it took all day on the 30th to get the ship not more than five miles from their last anchoring place. Contrary winds and bad weather prevented the *Resolution* leaving the bay until May 11th when she stood out to sea. After getting underway Captain Cook directed a course to Queen Charlotte's Sound, where he expected to find the *Adventure*. After a fine beginning the weather quickly deteriorated with a dark sky. This made them clew up the sails and presently waterspouts were seen. Four rose and spent themselves between the ship and the land, the fifth was on the seaward side, and the sixth some three miles away. Its progressive motion was to the north-east not in a straight, but a crooked line, and passed within fifty yards of the ships stern. Its diameter was judged to be between fifty or sixty feet at the base ; that is the sea within that space was much agitated, and foamed up to a great height. Some of the crew said they saw a bird in the one nearest the ship ; which was whirled round like 'the fly of a jack' as it was carried upwards.

In passing from Cape Farewell to Cape Stephens, Cook had a better view of the coast than on his earlier voyage. He saw a spacious bay and believed that this was the same that Captain Tasman anchored in on December 18th,1642, by him called Murderer's Bay, when some of his men were killed by the natives.

On arriving off Queen Charlotte's Sound, everyone was pleased to observe signals from the *Adventure*. The wind dropped, so the *Resolution* had to be towed in by the boats. At noon Lieutenant Kemp of the *Adventure* came on board and informed Cook that the ship had been there about six weeks. On getting anchored next to the *Adventure,* Captain Furneaux came on board to give Cook an account of his circumstances from the time the ships parted.. After losing sight of the *Resolution* in the thick fog in February, he had hauled up south-east and kept firing a four-pounder every half-hour ; but received no reply. He kept to the course they steered before the fog. He tacked and stood to the westward, to cruise to the place where they had last seen her, but a very heavy gale blew them off course. When the gale abated they had cruised for three days as near to the place as they could get, but giving up hope of joining company again, they bore off to winter quarters, some fourteen hundred leagues distant, through a sea entirely unknown ; rationing the water allowances to one quart per day. They witnessed the Southern Lights, but saw only one iceberg after parting company with Captain Cook's ship.

On March 9th they sighted land which Furneaux took to be the South Cape, as named by Tasman. Further along the coast, next day, as the ship was four miles from land, the first lieutenant was sent with the great cutter to see if there was a suitable landing place. A storm blew up and for a time contact with the cutter was lost. On its return they reported that they had landed with great difficulty, and saw evidence where natives had been, but did not see anyone. After sailing across the bay, experiencing bad weather, they anchored in a suitable place where they could obtain water, and stayed for four days, gathering wood and water. They did, however, see some huts which appeared to be of only a temporary construction. Wooding and watering completed, they set off again, passing Maria's Island on March 16th. Inclement weather prevented them nearing the coast, so Captain Furneaux had decided to make for New Zealand.

On April 7th they anchored near Motuara Island and spent two days clearing space for tents to house the sick, having several cases of the scurvy on board. On top of the island was a post, erected by the *Endeavour* people, with her name and time of departure on it. On the 9th sixteen natives in three canoes came and the English negotiated to obtain some fish. One of the natives had an object which was carefully wrapped up. On being persuaded to show it to the officers, it was found to be the head of a man lately killed. They remembered Tupia, when he had come with Captain Cook. In the afternoon they returned with fish and fern roots, which they exchanged for nails etc. It was with great pleasure, when on May 17th Furneaux saw the *Resolution*.

Captain Cook now decided to sail east between the latitudes of forty-one degrees and forty-six degrees south. He ordered Captain Furneaux to prepare his ship for sea. After planting some vegetables and showing the natives how they would be to their benefit, Cook was ready to sail by June 2nd. Cruising east, he observed the largest seal he had ever seen ; they fired at it but after an hours chase, couldn't catch it. On sending some men in the boat to cut some wood, they were chased by natives in a large double canoe. No harm was done and trading with the natives continued. Most visiting parties asked for Tupia and seemed very concerned to learn that he was dead.

Captain Cook now intended to voyage until he arrived at 140" or 135" west ; then, provided that no land was discovered, to proceed to Tahiti ; then back to Motuara by the shorter route ; and after taking in wood and water, to proceed to the south and explore all the unknown parts of the sea between the meridian of New Zealand and Cape Horn In case of separation, Tahiti was chosen as the place of rendezvous. Captain Furneaux was told that, in that event he was to remain until August 20th, and if not joined with Cook by that date, to proceed to Queen Charlotte's Sound, where he was to wait until November 20th.

Captain Cook, being a religious man, was displeased to find the morals of the New Zealand men and women had not improved. Some of the men induced the women to offer their bodies to the sailors in exchange for a spike-nail, even without regard to the privacy which decency required.

On July 29th Cook made enquiries on board the *Adventure* regarding the health of the crew. He was informed that the cook was dead and about twenty of her best men were laid up with the scurvy or flux. The *Resolution* had only three men on the sick list and Cook was unable to understand the disparity between the two vessels.

Land was seen on August 11th ; this was found to be an island with coconut trees. Cook named it Resolution Island. No time was spent exploring this island because of the state of the *Adventure's* crew. Cook resolved to lose no time in making for Tahiti. In the evening another small island was seen, which Cook named Doubtful Island. The next morning another small island was seen, but it had a coral reef and Cook named it after Captain Furneaux. The reef alerted the commander to the danger that could lie ahead and he sent out the cutter with an officer and seven men with orders to keep as far ahead of the ships with a light at her mast-head, as a signal that could be distinguished, which they were to make in case of any danger. The following morning found them in clear seas and the cutter was hoisted aboard and the ships steered to Tahiti.

Captain Cook informed Captain Furneaux that he intended to put into Oaiti-piha Bay, near the south-east end of Tahiti, to get what refreshments they could. At day-break the next morning the ships were found to be in a dangerous situation, being not more than half-a-league from a reef. The wind dropped and the boats had to be got out to tow the ships off, but all their efforts were not enough to prevent the ships being carried nearer the reef. A number of canoes came off, bringing a little fish, a few coconuts and other fruits, which they exchanged for nails, beads, etc. Most of them recognised Cook and asked after Mr Banks and others who had been on

Cook's earlier voyage, but no one asked for Tupia. A gap was eventually found in the reef, but the water was too narrow. The current here was very strong and Cook faced the prospect of a shipwreck as the *Resolution* was drawn along with it. The anchor was dropped, but before it took hold, the ship was in less than a fathom of water, striking at every fall of the sea. Eventually the tide changed direction and a breeze from the land carried the ships to safety, although the *Adventure* lost three anchors, a coasting cable and two hawsers. During this crisis a number of natives were aboard the ships, but did not seem the least concerned about the situation.

On the 17th the ships anchored in Oaiti-piha Bay. The natives came in great numbers, crowding the ships and trading with coconuts, bananas, plantains, apples, yams and other roots. To several who called themselves chiefs, Cook gave presents of axes, shirts and other articles. In the afternoon Cook, with Captain Furneaux inspected the watering-place and was met with great civility by the natives. Hogs were unobtainable, although many had been seen about the homes of the natives ; but Cook was informed that they belonged to the king, or Earee de Hi, as he was called. Many who called themselves Earees came on board and one of them was caught thieving and handing the stolen goods out of the quarter-gallery. Cook turned them all off the ship and had two muskets fired above the head or the so-called king, who took to the water. A boat was sent out to capture him, but as they got near the shore, they were pelted with stones. As the boast crew were unharmed, Cook went in another boat and ordered a great gun, loaded with ball, to be fired along the coast. This made the natives retreat and two canoes were taken by the English, one of which contained a small boy who was very scared. Cook gave him some beads and set him ashore. A few hours later all were friends again and the canoes were returned to the natives.

In the evening one or two Tahitians made enquiries about Tupia. On being told the manner of his death they were satisfied. They informed Cook that Toutaha, the regent of the greater peninsula of Tahiti, had been killed in a battle, which was fought between the two kingdoms about five months before ; and that Otoo was the reigning prince. Tabouri Tamaide, and several more of the principal friends of the English about Matavai, fell in the battle, as also did a great number of the common people ; but at present a peace subsisted between the two kingdoms.

In the evening of the 20th, a musket belonging to a guard on shore was stolen. The commander was present and sent some men after the thief. However, some of the natives, of their own accord, pursued him and knocked him down, took the gun from him and returned it to the guard.

As Cook was making ready to sail to Matavai, he was informed that Waheatoua, the ruling prince, was come to the neighbourhood and wanted to see him. Early the next day, Cook, Furneaux, Forster and a party of natives set out to meet him, encountering him about a mile from the landing-place, towards which he was making, but on seeing Cook's party, he stopped and sat on a seat. Cook and the prince recognised each other at once, having met in 1769. After the first salutations were over Waheatoua seated Cook on the same seat with himself. He enquired after others whom he remembered from the previous voyage and asked how long the visitors were staying. Cook told him no longer than the next day. He seemed sorry and asked that they stay some months and at last came down to five days, promising that they would have hogs in plenty. Cook did not have much faith in the promise. The commander made the prince presents consisting of a broad axe, spike-nails, a shirt, a sheet, knives, looking-glasses, medals, beads, etc. In return he ordered a pretty good hog to be carried to the ship. After returning to the ship for dinner, they again visited the ruler, making him more presents. In return he gave Cook and Captain Furneaux a hog each. Some others were got by exchanges at the trading-places, so that they got in that day, as much fresh pork as gave the crews of both ships a meal.

They put to sea on the 24th with a light land breeze. Many canoes accompanied them out to sea with coconuts and other fruits ; and did not leave until they had disposed of all their cargo. The fruits they had obtained there greatly contributed to the recovery of the *Adventure's* sick men. Lieutenant Pickersgill with the cutter was left behind to purchase hogs ; as several had promised to bring some down. About noon the next day, he returned with eight pigs, which he got at Ohiti-piha. He had spent the night at Ohedea, being well entertained by Ereti, the chief of the district. In the evening they reached Matavai Bay. Before they could get to anchor the decks were crowded by natives.

After having given directions to put the tents for the reception of the sick, coopers, sail-makers, and the guard, Cook set off for Oparree ; accompanied by Furneaux, Forster and others, Maritata (a chief), and his wife. As soon as they landed they were conducted to Otoo, their king, whom they found seated on the ground under the shade of a tree, with an immense crowd around him. Presents were made to the king and some of his attendants, in return they offered cloth, which Cook refused, telling them what he had given was for *tiya* (friendship). Otoo promised that they would have some hogs the next day, but took much persuasion to board the ship, as he said he was afraid of the guns. He was about thirty years of age, six foot in height and a fine personable man. All his subjects appeared before him stripped to the waist.

The following morning, Otoo, attended by a tribe of his subjects went on board the ship, having just sent a large quantity of cloth, fruits, a hog, and two large fish. Cook made presents to them all, took them home to Oparree and Captain Furneaux presented Otoo with a male and a female goat. Otoo made no further visits to the *Resolution* and the *Adventure*. Cook noted that when Otoo came into the cabin, Ereti and some of his friends who were sitting there, stripped in great haste. This was the only respect they paid him, for they never rose from their seats, nor made any other obeisance. On returning to Oparree, some of the crew entertained Otoo with bagpipes, which he liked very much, and hornpipes and country dances, which all the natives tried to emulate.

On August 29th Cook paid Otoo a further visit and presented him with some gifts, including a broad-sword ; at the sight of which he was so intimidated, that it took Cook some time to persuade him to buckle it on ; where he allowed it to remain for a very short time, before he sent it out of his sight. Soon after they were conducted to the theatre in which they were entertained to a play, featuring dancing and comedy. It was performed by the king's sister and five men. The visitors did not understand what it was about, but it seemed to relate to that immediate time, as Cook's name was frequently mentioned.

At two o'clock the following morning Cook was alarmed by a cry of murder, and a great commotion on shore. He suspected that it was caused by some of his own men and sent on shore an armed boat to bring off any of his crew, as none were missing from the *Resolution,* he sent to the *Adventure* and the post on shore to see who was absent. The boat soon returned with three marines and a seaman. Some others belonging to the *Adventure* were also taken, and all were placed under confinement until the next morning, when they were punished. Cook could not get a confession from any of them and he assumed that the trouble had been caused by their sexual romps with the women.

The king had fled inland, being scared by the nights rioting. Cook had to wait some time to pay his farewell respects. His next destination was the island of Huaheine, which was reached the next day. The night was spent making short boards under the northern end of the island. At daylight on September 3rd, they made sail for the harbour of Owharre, in which the *Resolution* anchored about nine o'clock. As the wind blew out of the harbour, Cook chose to turn in by the southern channel, it being the widest. the *Resolution* turned in very well, but the *Adventure*, missing stays, got ashore on the north side of the channel. The *Resolution's* launch was sent to help and she was got off again, without receiving any damage.

Soon after arriving in Tahiti, they were informed that a ship, about the size of the *Resolution*, had been in Owhaiurua harbour near the south-east end of the island ; where she remained about three weeks. 'The Tahitians complained about a disease communicated to them by the people in this ship,' wrote Captain Cook, 'which they said affected the head, throat and stomach, and at length killed them. They seemed to dread it much, and continually enquiring if we had it. This ship they distinguished by the name of *Pahai an Pep-pe* (ship of Peppe), and called the disease *Apa-no-Pep-pe*, just as they called the venereal disease *Apa-no-Pretane* (English disease), though they, to a man, say it was brought to the island by M.de Bourganville [1768] ; but I have already observed they thought M.de Bourganville came from *Pretane,* as well as every other ship that touched this isle. Were it not for this assertion of the natives, and none of Captain Wallis's people being affected with the venereal disease, either while they were at Otheite, or after they left it, I should have concluded that, long before these islanders were visited by Europeans, this, or some disease that is near akin to it, had existed among them ; for I have heard them speak of people dying of a disorder which we interpreted to be the pox, before that period ; but be this as it will, it is now far less common among them than it was in the year 1769, when I first visited these isles. They say they can cure it, and so it fully appears ; for notwithstanding most of my people made pretty free with the women, very few of them were afterwards affected by the disorder ; and those who were had it in so slight a manner that it was easily removed ; but amongst the natives, whenever it turns to pox, they tell us it is incurable.'

On prostitution, Cook wrote : ' That there are prostitutes here, as well as in other countries, is very true, perhaps more in proportion, and such were those who came aboard our ships to our people, and frequented the post we had on shore. By seeing these mix indiscriminately with those of a different turn, even of the first rank, one is, at first inclined to think that they are all disposed the same way, and that the only difference is the price. But the truth is, the woman who becomes a prostitute, does not seem, in their opinion, to have committed a crime of so deep a dye as to exclude her from the esteem and society of the community in general,'

Needles to say, Captain Cook, being a religious man of high morals, did not entertain these women.

Cook was reunited with Oree, the chief of that island, who shed tears of joy as he embraced the captain. He promised they would have all their needs supplied, and many hogs were obtained, as well as fruit and other necessities.

Mr Sparrman, imprudently went botanising on his own, and was set upon by two natives, who stripped him of all his clothes, apart from his trousers. Another native, finding the botanist half-naked, covered him with a piece of cloth and conducted him to the trading-place. The chief's help was sought to punish the men concerned. These proceedings created great alarm among the natives, and when the chief insisted on going aboard ship with Captain Cook, they wept and entreated him not to go. On his safe return a great crowd rejoiced to see him safe.

On September 7th, Cook, Captain Furneaux and Mr Forster paid a farewell visit to Oree, who embraced the commander with tears in his eyes. They gave the king some useful presents and a small copper plate, on which were engraved these words : *Anchored here, His Britannic Majesty's ships Resolution and Adventure, September 1773*. As the ships set sail, Oree came off and informed Cook that the two culprits, who had robbed Mr Sparrman, had been caught and asked Cook to return to see them punished ; but this could not be done as the *Resolution* was just under sail, and the *Adventure* already out of the harbour. Oree stayed on board until they were a full half league out to sea During their stay at the small but fertile island of Huaheine, they procured to both ships not less than three hundred hogs, besides fowl and fruits ; and had they stayed longer, might have got many more, for none of these commodities were seemingly diminished, but appeared everywhere in as great abundance as ever.

Captain Furneaux had taken on board a young man named Omai, a native of

THE LANDING AT MIDDLEBURGH, ONE OF THE FRIENDLY ISLANDS.
Palms are offered as a sign of friendship.

Ulitea, where he had some property, of which he had been dispossessed by the people of Bolabola. At first Cook thought that this was unwise, but he later acknowledged that Omai was an excellent man

Arriving at the harbour of Ohamaneno, in Ulietea, the usual crowd of natives came off in their canoes to trade. Everyone asked after Tupia and the manner of his death. On being told the circumstances they accepted it philosophically. A formal visit was paid to the chief, Oreo, and the usual presents made. Hogs were received in return. During their stay the officers were entertained by visits to the theatre. Captain Cook was introduced to Oo-oorou, the principal chief of all the isle.

One morning Captain Cook was surprised that no natives came off to the ship as was usual. Two men belonging to the *Adventure* had stayed on shore all night, contrary to orders. Cook's first conjecture was that the natives had stripped them, and were now afraid to come near them, in case they should take some steps to revenge the insult. Cook and Furneaux went to the chief's house, but found it empty and the neighbourhood deserted. the two men from the *Adventure* appeared and said that they had been treated civilly by the natives, but could give no reason for their precipitate flight. All Cook could learn from the few natives who dared come near him, was that several were killed, others wounded by the English guns. This caused the commander some alarm for the safety of his men in the boats, which he had sent to Otawa to obtain plantains, fearing that some disturbance had happened on that island. He resolved to see the chief, but it took quite some time and effort to catch up with him. It appears that the natives, observing the boats departing, thought that the men in them were deserting and that Cook would take some violent means to recover them. When he assured them that the boats would be returning, they seemed cheerful and satisfied, and to a man, denied that anyone was hurt, either of their own, or the ships people.

When they sailed from the isle, Captain Cook took on board with him a native of Bolabola, who was seventeen years of age. Named Oedidee, he was a near relation of Opoony, the chief of that island.

Leaving Ulietea, the ships steered to the west, inclining to the south ; to get clear of the tracks of former navigators, and to get into the latitudes of the islands of Middleburg and Amsterdam, for Cook intended to run as far as these islands, before he hauled up to New Zealand. Middleburg was reached on October 1st at two o'clock in the afternoon. Next day they found a suitable anchorage and Cook made friends with Tioony, a chief who had come aboard. This chief conducted them to a little creek where the boat could land easily. An immense crowd of people welcomed them ashore. Tioony took them to his house and Cook ordered the bagpipes to be played. In return the chief directed three young women to sing a song, 'which they did with very good grace,' and having made each of them a present, this immediately set all the women in the circle singing. Although the natives were very friendly, no fruit or roots, or animals could be obtained, so Cook resolved to leave the island after a few days.

The ships sailed on to the island which Tasman called Amsterdam and anchored in Van Dieman's Road. The natives came off with cloth and matting which the sailors exchanged for their clothes. Cook foresaw that this would soon prove a disadvantage to them and forbid any further trade. When the natives found that the sailors would only trade for eatables, they brought off coconuts and bananas in abundance, some fowls and pigs, all of which were exchanged for nails and pieces of cloth, even old rags were enough for a pig or a fowl.

A chief named Attago soon attached himself to Captain Cook, who went ashore with Captain Furneaux, Mr Forster and other officers, to be given a guided tour of the island, in which they visited a place of worship, where they were addressed by a elderly man, whom Cook took to be a priest. They had not the least idea what he said, but each time he paused, Cook nodded his head, when the man would continue. The island was seen to be very fertile, and the cultivation well-planned and laid out in plantations. On returning to the shore they found Mr Wales had taken off his shoes and socks to wade ashore, when they had been immediately snatched and made off with. Attago soon found out the thief and the footwear was recovered.

An old chief came on board and was invited to dinner. Cook noticed that Attago would not sit down and eat before him, but went to the other end of the table and ate with his back turned towards the old chief. Cook also met another high-ranking person, whom Cook understood to be the Areeke, or king of the island. The man showed no reaction to the explorers and so Cook took him to be stupid. He was wrong on that point and later the king sent a present of twenty baskets of roasted bananas, some bread and yams, and a roasted pig of about twenty pounds weight.

On October 7th, the ships got under sail, but not before one of the coasting cables had parted in the middle, through rubbing on the rocks, losing them an anchor. Cook described the two types of canoe ; the single ones were about thirty feet in length, and the double ones, or catamarans, were about sixty feet in length. The natives were copper-coloured and the women most agreeable ; in general they appeared to be modest, although there was no shortage of the other kind ; and as he had some sailors with venereal complaints on board, he took all possible care to prevent the disease being transmitted to them.

The ships now proceeded towards New Zealand, where Cook intended to anchor in Queen Charlotte's Sound, to take in wood and water and then to go on making further discoveries to the south and east. Passing the island of Pilstart, discovered by Tasman, on the 8th, New Zealand was sighted thirteen days later. Sailing along the coast, the *Resolution* lost its fore-top-gallant mast in a gale. It was also during this gale that the *Adventure*, failing to observe a signal, was separated once more, but was reunited on the 24th. Unfavourable weather and gales prevented a landing and in a violent storm the two ships were again parted. On the morning of the 28th, the *Adventure* was again seen four or five miles to the leeward, but on the 29th the result yet of another gale caused a final separation of the ships. As the *Resolution* approached the Sound a new inlet was discovered on the east side of Cape Teerawhitte. Being tired with beating against the north-west winds, Cook resolved to put in there and anchored in twelve fathoms water. A shift in the wind to the south meant they were just able to lead out of the bay, and then bore away for the Sound under all the sail they could set. They hauled up into the Sound just after dark and anchored in eighteen fathoms between the White Rocks and the north-west shore. Next morning the gale abated and they ran up into Ship Cove, where they did not find the *Adventure,* as was expected.

After mooring the ship, the first task was to unbend all the sails, there not been one but needed repair. The empty water casks were ordered ashore to be repaired, cleaned and filled ; tents to be set up for the sail-makers, coopers, etc. The following day they began to caulk the ship's sides and deck, overhaul her rigging, cut wood for fuel, and set up the smiths' forge to repair the ironwork. Some trading with the natives produced a quantity of fish. There were some incidents of thieving, as was common with most of the natives of the South Seas, although Cook said the New Zealanders were far less addicted to thieving than the other islanders these southern islands. A few of the officers, visiting some natives in their habitation, saw among them some human thigh-bones from which the flesh had been recently picked. It was the custom to eat their enemies from other tribes who were killed in battle.

INTO THE UNKNOWN

IT WAS November 23rd before the *Resolution could* put to sea again and Captain Cook resolved not to leave the coast without looking for the *Adventure.* With this in view he stood over for Cape Teerawhitte, and afterwards made runs along the shore, from point to point, to Cape Palliser, firing guns every half-hour, but to no avail. By November 26th, Cook had given up all hopes of seeing the *Adventure* again ; he then set his sights for further exploration of the southern part of the Pacific Ocean. He had the satisfaction to find that not a man was dejected, or thought the dangers they had yet to go through were in the least increased by being alone; 'but being as cheerfully proceeding to the south, or wherever I might lead them, as if the *Adventure,* or even more ships, had been in our company.' Thanks to the fruit, vegetables and other food
they had received while in these islands, the crew and personnel of the *Resolution* were in a fit condition.

Now they sailed towards the Antarctic, once more in a vain search for the mystical Southern Continent. On December 12th they encountered the first iceberg. Sailing through ice flows, they saw seventeen icebergs on the 15th. Captain Cook took care to keep the wind on the beam, so that it might be in his power to turn back nearly on the same track, should his course be interrupted by any danger. He considered the loose ice flows to be more dangerous than the icebergs. The ship took some hard knocks from large pieces of loose ice ; and there was fog with the danger of hitting an iceberg. After nearly hitting one of those floating monstrosities, which Cook thought of as islands, Cook decided to get more to the north. Snow, sleet, and rain were the conditions they experienced the most ; the snow freezing to the rigging so loading it that they had enough to do to get the top-sails down to double the reef ; as they sailed a course south-east. By Christmas Eve Cook had turned his course north-east, encountering on that day one hundred icebergs. Returning for a third time to the Antarctic Polar Circle, they thought they had sighted land, but it turned out to be only clouds. On January 30th, 1774, they reached field ice, extending east and west far beyond the reach of their sight. Ninety-seven ice hills, some resembling mountains, were counted. It was Captain Cook's ambition to

RESOLUTION BAY IN THE MARQUESAS ISLANDS.

not only go further than any man had been before, but as far as possible for man to go. Cook and others on board were of the opinion that the ice field stretched as far as the South Pole.

Captain Cook now decided to sail towards Tahiti, where he hoped to find the *Adventure* ; but on the way there to search for other islands, such as Easter Island or Davis's Island, whose situation was well-known with so little certainty. During February, Cook was taken ill with bilious colic, which confined him to his bed. The management of the ship was vested in Mr Cooper, the first officer, who conducted her to the satisfaction of the commander. At 8 o'clock in the morning of Marcg 11th, Easter Island was sighted from the mast. The adventurers were met with a friendly reception, but the natives were expert thieves. Captain Cook was weak from his recent illness and found difficulty in walking, so Lieutenants Pickersgill and Edgecombe went on an exploration of the island, viewing the great stone statues. The island proved to be barren and water was scarce and of poor quality, so Cook determined to make his stay there a short one ; accordingly the anchor was raised on March 16th, and a course set for the Marquesas. During the passage to the Marquesas, Cook had a reoccurrence of his illness, but this time not so violent. The first island was seen on April 6th, which was a new discovery, Cook naming it Hood's Island, after the young man who first saw it ; the second was that of St.Pedro ; the third La Dominica ; and the fourth St.Christina. They were first discovered by Mendana in 1595, and Cook searched for Mendana's Port, which he found, but was prevented from entering this refuge by a strong wind off the high land. Natives came off in canoes and while attempting to trade, would steal anything they could get their hands on. During the theft of a steel stantion, the thief was shot Two others in the same canoe leaped overboard. One man sat baling blood and water out of the canoe, with a kind of hysteric laugh. Another, about fourteen years of age, looked at the corpse with a dejected expression. Cook believed he was the son. the other natives fled to the shore. Cook went out in the boat and gave them nails etc. Friendlier relations were established and some trading took place, but it became evident that the supplies would not be plentiful.

Cook continued his course towards Tahiti and on April 17th a string of islets connected together by a reef of coral rocks, was encountered. Two boats were sent on shore, but the natives gave the men a cool reception. After passing other low-lying islands, Tahiti was reached on April 21st and

THE TAHITIAN FLEET ASSEMBLED AT OPARRE.
Note the multiple hull construction of these fighting Ivahas.

they anchored the following morning in Matavai Bay. Otoo, the king, and other chiefs, renewed their acquaintance and brought as presents ten large hogs and fruit. Cook extended his intended stay, to make repairs to the ship, the empty casks and sails.

During his stay Cook witnessed a great naval review ; the vessels of war consisted of no less than one hundred-and-sixty large double canoes, very well equipped, manned and armed. There was also one hundred-and-seventy sail of smaller catamarans, all with a little house on them, and rigged with a mast and sail, which the war canoes had not. Cook was given to understand that the force was assembled to go against Eimeo, whose chief had thrown off the yolk of Tahiti, declaring an independence.

A native was caught stealing a water casck and was put in irons aboard ship, in which situation Otoo and other chiefs saw him. Otoo begged that he be set free, but Cook refused, taking him on shore and tying him to a post. Cook pointed out to Otoo that his people always paid for what they got ; and that it was wrong for the natives to steal from the visitors, who were their friends. Cook said that if his men went against his orders they were punished and he intended to do the same with the thief. In spite of Otoos pleas, the man was given two dozen lashes with the cat-o-nine-tails, which he bore with great firmness, and was then set free.

There was another unpleasant incident before Cook left Tahiti. This concerned the theft of a musket from a sentry who was asleep at his post on shore. At first Cook made a big thing of trying to get it back. In the end he gave up, considering it not worth the fuss and effort. Shortly after the musket was returned by some natives, together with some other items which had been stolen, but which the visitors had not yet missed.

Old Oberea, who had been thought of as queen of the islands, paid Cook a visit on May 12th. Presents were exchanged and, in the evening, he entertained Oberea and her retinue to a fireworks display.

At one o'clock in the afternoon of May 15th, the *Resolution* anchored in the north entrance of O'Wharre harbour, in the island of Huaheine. Cook renewed his acquaintance with Oree, the chief. During the stay there they received bread-fruit, coconuts, etc., more than they could well consume, but not enough hogs. Cook set the smiths to produce nails, and other items to bargain with on other islands. On the 23rd the ship put to sea, steering for the island of Ulietea, which was reached the next day. Captain Cook's old friend Oreeo came off, with others, bringing presents. Ulietea was

Oedidee's native island and he chose to take leave of his English friends, which he did in a very emotional manner.

Passing Howe Island, and an unknown one, which Cook named Palmerston, land was seen on June 20th. Going on shore the explorers received a very hostile reception, the commander being narrowly missed by a spear. Because of this incident he named it Savage Island. Travelling west-south-west, a string of islands was seen. These islands were of the Tonga group to which Cook had given the name of the Friendly Islands. During a watering party on shore, Mr Clerke's gun was snatched. Mr Forster had also had his fowling-piece stolen. Cook thought it necessary to send the marines on shore and to fire the ships guns. When the marines landed Mr Clerke's gun was brought back.

After leaving the Friendly Islands, and calling on July 1st at Turtle Island, a brisk gale carried the ship towards the great Cyclades, which was seen on the 15th. Cook explored the coast for some days, coming to anchor in the island of Mallicollo. This part of the world turned out to be unfriendly, but Cook continued his survey.

On September 4th, land was seen and the ship stood in the following morning, to be immediately surrounded by canoes filled with unarmed natives. A good watering-place was found and plenty of food was obtained. These natives did not steal, but they did not have an abundance of refreshments.

By the beginning of October a gale sprang up, which rendered further survey of the group impossible. They therefore bore away for New Zealand. On the 10th an island of good height was seen, Cook naming it Norfolk Island. New Zealand was reached seven days later. The ship was anchored in Ship Cove, and repairs were begun. The natives said that a ship like the *Resolution* had been lost in the strait, and that some of the people got on shore, when the natives stole their clothes, for which several were shot. Afterwards, when the sailors could fire no longer, the natives killed them with their clubs and spears, and ate them. The natives declared that they themselves had no part in the matter, which occurred at some distance along the coast.

The *Resolution* left Queen Charlotte's Sound for the last time on November 10th. Cook resolved that having a strong ship and a healthy crew, he would accomplish some more work before returning home. He made a survey of the coasts round Tierra del Fuego. The ship was brought to anchor on December 20th, in a harbour which Cook named Christmas Sound. Many wild fowl were shot here, so Christmas Dinner consisted of roast and boiled geese, and goose in any form which it could be presented, accompanied, in the cabin, by Madeira.

Rounding Cape Horn on the 29th, a course was steered to the Straits of Lemaire, and Success Bay to ascertain if the *Adventure* had called there, but no trace was found. A man named Willis spotted land on January 13th, 1775. At first it was thought to be an iceberg, but it turned out to be an island and it was named after Willis. After naming Bird Island, the Isle of Georgia, and Southern Thule, a course was set for the Cape of Good Hope, and on March 21st, the *Resolution* anchored in Table Bay, where a letter from Captain Furneaux awaited Captain Cook. This confirmed that ten men, under the charge of Mr Rowe, had been sent on shore in New Zealand on December 17th, 1773, to gather greens. As they did not return in the evening, another boat was sent, under the command of Lieutenant Burney, when the mutilated remains of the cutters crew were discovered, some parts scattered along the beach, and others carefully packed with fern, in baskets, evidently intended for the oven. After this misfortune, the *Adventure* sailed for the Cape of Good Hope, and then to England.

The *Resolution* anchored in Portsmouth on July 30th, 1775, having been absent from England three years and eighteen days, and during that time had lost only four men, and only one by sickness.

It says much for the quality of his men who were willing to help him in his extended explorations, amid such hardships which they were bound to endure. It says much too for the attributes of their leader. One of his crew summed him up as follows : 'He was strict and hot-tempered in that the slightest disobedience by an officer or a seaman upset him completely, no one ever dared to contradict him. At times he was very affable towards the crew ; if any of the crew fell ill Captain Cook always enquired after him and directed the medical men to attend him. Temperance was one of his chief virtues, I never saw him drunk. On Saturdays he was as a rule more friendly than on other days ; he would drink a glass of punch to the health of all beautiful women and maidens. Never once was there the slightest suspicion of his, having intercourse with the native women ; at Tahiti and Hawaii, where everyone yielded to the attractions of the women folk, he always remained pure and clean.'

On his return Captain Cook was honoured, receiving post rank, and being nominated a Captain in Greenwich Hospital, which would have enabled him to spend the rest of his life in honourable retirement. In February 1776 he was elected a Fellow of the Royal Society. On the evening of his admission, March 7th, a paper was read in which he gave a full account of the various means he had used to ensure the health of his crew.

THE FINAL VOYAGE

MEN had long mooted the possibility of a north-west passage around the coast of North America into the Pacific Ocean, so that China, Japan and the East Indies might be reached by a route shorter than by the Cape of Good Hope. In 1745 an Act of Parliament was passed, offering a reward of £20,000 to any ship belonging to any of His Majesty's subjects which should discover such a passage. Numerous bold adventurers, from Frobisher, in 1576, had made the effort. The British Government sent out Captain Middleton in 1741 ; and Captains Smith and Moore four years later. In 1773, at the instigation of Daines Barrington, an influential member of the Royal Society, Lord Sandwich sent out Captain Constantine John Phipps [afterwards created Lord Mulgrave, 1790] , with the *Racehorse* and the *Carcase,* which was commanded by Captain Lutwidge, having on board a young boy called Horatio Nelson. Captain Phipps returned having been unable to penetrate the wall of ice which barred his progress.

Asked his opinion by Lord Sandwich at a dinner with Sir Hugh Palliser, Mr Stephens and others, and coming to the point of fixing on a fit person to take command of an expedition to find a north-west passage, Captain Cook rose to his feet and declared himself ready to take command. The date was set for February 10th,1776 ; the usual plan of search was to be reversed by sailing round Cape Horn, and then north, attempting to work its way through the Bering Strait eastward into the Atlantic. The *Resolution* and the *Adventure,* those Whitby-built vessels which had proved their worth, were again chosen, with Cook in command of the former, with John Gore as his first lieutenant, and the other to Captain Clerke, while Lieutenant King went out again as second lieutenant of the *Resolution.* Also on Captain Cook's ship were Mr William Anderson, the surgeon, who took charge of the department of natural history, and Mr Webber, the artist, to make sketches of any scenes of interest. With Captain Clerke was Mr Bayley, the astronomer. The officers of the *Resolution* were John Gore, James King and John Wiliamson, lieutenants ; William Bligh [later notoriously famous as captain of the mutinous *Bounty*] master ; Molesworth Philips, lieutenant Royal Marines. Those of the *Discovery* were James Burney, John Rickham, lieutenants ; Thomas Edgar, master ; John Law, surgeon. Great care was taken with the fitting out of the ships, some months passing before they were ready for the sea.

Captain Cook received his orders on July 6th,1776. His chief object was to find a passage from the Pacific into the Atlantic. He was to leave the Cape of Good Hope early in November, and first to search for certain islands, seen by the French, south of the Mauritius, but not to spend too much time in looking for them, or examining them, but to proceed to Tahiti, touching at New Zealand, should he find it necessary to refresh his crews. Then he was to proceed to the coast of New Albion, avoiding where possible, any Spanish settlements. Arrived in the Frozen Ocean, he was to examine all channels and inlets likely to lead eastwards ; to take possession in the name of the king any territory on which he might land, previously undiscovered. He was to winter at the Russian settlement of St.Peter and St.Paul in Kamschatka, and to return in the spring to the north.

Captain Cook, with Omai, who had come to England with Captain Furneaux, sailed from Plymouth on July 11th, but owing to unfavourable winds, did not leave the Scilly Isles until the 16th. Captain Clerke had not yet arrived on board the *Discovery,* so her departure was delayed until August. He was ordered to proceed to the Cape of Good Hope, there to join the *Resolution.* In the meantime Captain Cook touched at Teneriffe, where he found plenty of supplies, sailing again on August 4th. On the 10th, Bonavista, one of the Cape de Verde Islands was seen. Just then breakers were seen directly under the ships lee and for a few minutes she was in grave danger. Having weathered them she stood for Port Praya, hoping to find the *Discovery* there ; as she was not the *Resolution* did not go in, but continued for the Cape, where she was anchored on October 18th ; having crossed the line on September 1st, observing the usual ceremonies. At the Cape provisions were obtained and the tents were set up on shore for the astronomical instruments. A fierce gale ripped the tents to pieces, the instruments narrowly avoiding damage.

The *Discovery* joined up again with Cook, entering the bay on November 10th. Like the *Resolution* she required caulking, which delayed the expedition until the end of the month. A course was steered south-east. Before long a heavy squall carried away the *Resolution's* mizzen-topmast ;

and a mountainous sea rolled the ship so much that it was difficult to save the animals on board ; owing to this and the cold, several goats and sheep died.

On December 10th two islands were seen about five leagues apart ; they were some of those described by French navigators in 1772. Cook gave the name of Prince Edward's to the two he had just discovered. On the 24th an island of considerable height was seen and the following day others were observed. As the ships cruised along the coast, a terrific sea rolled in on the shore, placing them in great danger. Although it was mid-summer the weather was very cold. On Christmas Day they found an harbour where both ships found a good anchorage, plenty of water, innumerable penguins and other birds, as also seals which were so unused to human beings that they allowed themselves to be knocked on the head without showing any resistance. A bottle was discovered containing a document left by Kerguelen, the Frenchman, who had discovered this land at the end of 1773. The harbour was named Christmas Harbour in commemoration of the day they had entered it.

Leaving on the morning of the 28th, they continued along the coast in order to discover its position and extent ; they brought up in anothet harbour to escape a heavy gale, and then proceeded to the south towards Cape George. After leaving it on December 30th, a course was set for New Zealand. Thick fog was encountered so that for many days the ships could not see each other, though by constantly firing guns, they kept in touch. Cook determined to put in at Adventure Bay, in Van Dieman's Land. The ships were brought up in the bay on January 26th,1777. While wood was being cut, some natives appeared, completely naked. they came forward with perfect confidence, only one having a lance in his hand. A boar and a sow had been landed in the hope that they would breed, but as soon as the natives saw them, they seized them by the ears with the intention of killing them. Captain Cook, wishing to know the purpose of the lance which the one was carrying, the native set up a target and threw his weapon at it. He missed it so often that Omai, to show the superiority of the white man's weapons, fired his musket, at which the party fled, dropping some axes and other items which had been given to them. They ran towards where the *Adventure's* crew were cutting wood, when the officer, mistaking their intentions, fired a musket over their heads, which sent them off altogether.

Leaving Adventure Bay on January 30th, a furious gale was encountered, blowing from the south. At the same time the heat became almost insupportable, the thermometer rising from 70 degrees to near 90 Farenhite. The ships entered Queen Charlotte's Sound on February 12th, where the *Adventure* had suffered the terrible loss of some of her people. Before long several canoes acme alongside, but few would come on board, being fearful of receiving punishment for the murders. Captain Cook recognised many faces from his previous visit. He did his best to make them understand that he had not come to punish them, but wished to be friends with them as before.   However, he took the greatest precautions to prevent further trouble ; Mr King and other officers guarding working parties on shore. No boat was sent to any distance without being fully armed. Chiefs from other parts frequently visited the ships, among them one called Kahoora, who was pointed out as the leader of the crew that had attacked the *Adventure's* boat, and was said to have actually killed Mr Rowe, the officer in command. Much to the surprise of the natives, and to Omai, who asked that he be killed at once, Captain Cook declined seizing him, pointing out that he had declared an amnesty, and that no on would be punished, only if a similar outrage should occur the natives must expect the fearful vengeance of the English.

The ships left Queen Charlotte's Sound on February 25th and it was over a month later when the *Discovery* signalled land in the north-east. No landing seemed possible because of heavy surf. Some natives came off in canoes, but they were wary of coming on board. Omai was able to converse with them and discovered that their island was called Mangaia. The ships proceeded on March 30th and next day two islands were seen. Mr Gore and Mr Burney went on shore in the hopes of finding food for the livestock. Captain Cook was alarmed when the boat had not returned.   He felt somewhat reassured when the natives continued bringing coconuts etc., out to the ships. Late in the day the boats returned safely. It seems that the party had been jostled by a big crowd and conducted up an avenue of coconut palms, until they reached a body of men drawn up in two rows, armed with clubs resting on their shoulders. In the middle was a chief sitting crossed-legged, with coloured feathers in his ears. Then followed a sham fight between two men with clubs. Pressed by the vast crowd, the visitors became separated from each other and their pockets were picked. they were unable to get back to the boats until Omai let off some cartridges, which caused the crowd to scatter. Unable to obtain the food for the animals, a visit to the smaller island was made and all their needs were obtained.

A course was next set for Hervey Island, which Cook thought was uninhabited when he first visited it in 1773. He was surprised, therefore when a number of canoes came off. The occupants behaved in a wild and savage manner, so the ships sailed on for Palmerston's Island, where five boat crews cut food for the cattle. On leaving Palmerston's Island they passed Savage Island during the night of April 24th/25th, on the way to Annamook. On the evening of the 28th the ships anchored off Komango, one of the Friendly Islands, as Cook called Tonga. They were welcomed very civilly and Cook was introduced to Feenon as king of all the Friendly Isles. At Feenon's invitation Captain Cook agreed to go to Hapaee. The great chief came on board until the evening, when he took his departure with Omai, who had taken a great liking to him. They saw the volcanic mountain called Toofoa, which appeared active with flames and smoke.

Anchoring off Hapaee, the adventurers were deluged with provisions brought off by the natives. Going ashore at Feenon's invitation, the gentlemen were entertained by combats with clubs, boxing and wrestling. When darkness descended the visitors entertained the natives with a fireworks display. Cook was later visited by Poulaho, who arrived in a large sailing canoe. The natives declared that he was the real king of the Friendly Isles, much to the discomfort of Omai. At the request of Poulaho, Cook visited Tongataboo, where the ships were in considerable danger of driving on a low sandy island. A number of live animals were presented to the king and other people of importance, Cook instructing them to care for the livestock, allowing them to breed. A dangerous situation arose when the chiefs were dissatisfied with the allotment, and early next morning it was discovered that a kid and two turkey stags were missing. The captain put a guard on the king, declaring him a hostage, but inviting him on board for dinner. His subjects did not want him to go, but he went willingly, and on his return to shore, the missing livestock was restored. After this a party of officers went on shore making an excursion into the interior, with muskets and ammunition, and a number of items for barter, but the natives stripped them of everything.

It seems a high-handed and arrogant thing to do, taking the native king as an hostage, but it seems to have been a tactic which Cook adopted on his last voyage, and one which would ultimately lead to his downfall. There are

BOATS OF THE FRIENDLY ISLANDS.
Note the catamaran construction of the larger craft.

those who maintain that he had suffered a personality change by then. Certainly he seems to have become more cruel with the natives, punishing thieves, when caught, by shaving their heads and in some cases, cutting off their ears. On the other hand, the natives seem to have shown a more obdurate attitude. On one occasion, when Feenon was on board the *Resolution,* an inferior chief ordered all the people to retire from the English post on shore. Some ventured to return, when the chief took up a stick and beat them unmercifully. He struck one man with so much violence on the side of his face that the blood gushed out of his mouth and nostrils, and after lying down some time motionless he was removed in convulsions. The chief laughed when told that he had killed the man, seeming perfectly indifferent to the matter. Captain Cook little dreamed that those friendly natives, of whom he had thought so highly, and whom he praised as among the most humane people on earth, had, headed by Feenon, laid a plot for his destruction, and that of all his followers. Providentially the conspirators could not agree as to the method ; but all were equally eager to possess the stores of wealth the ships were thought to contain. Probably Feenon's pretended friendship with Omai was in the hope that he would have a ready tool in his hands. He had offered to make Omai a great chief if he would remain in Tonga, but Cook advised him not to accept the offer.

The native chiefs did their best to make Cook stay longer, but he set sail on July 17th with a course set for Tahiti. Land was not seen again until August 8th when the island of Toobonai was passed. Four days later Maitea was seen and shortly after Tahiti hove into view. Arrived once more in Tahiti, Captain Cook found that since his previous visit two Spanish ships had twice called in the bay, some of the Spaniards building a house and staying during the interim period. Some of them had died, the others went away when the ships returned. The natives pointed out the grave of the commodore of the two ships, who had died during the first visit. Two priests had been left as missionaries, but on the visit of the *Callao,* in 1775, they were found to be utterly disappointed, and determined to abandon their task, having made no progress in the conversion of the natives, and were so alarmed at the human sacrifices constantly taking place that they would only consent to remain under the protection of the Spanish garrison.

On August 23rd the ships were moved to Matavai Bay, and the following morning Captain Cook landed with Omaia and several officers, to pay his respects to the king, Otoo. After dinner Cook and some officers accompanied Otoo to Oparre, taking with them some poultry with which to stock the island.

While the ships lay at Matavai news was received that the people of Eimeo had revolted, and it was decided to send Towha, with a fleet against them, but before the fleet could sail it was necessary that a grand human sacrifice be made. The hapless victim had already been knocked on the head for the purpose. Captain Cook, wishing to confirm the truth of what he had heard, accompanied Omai to witness the ceremony. They were allowed to examine the victim, who was a man of middle age, and had been killed by a blow on the temple. Forty-nine skulls were counted in one heap, which by all appearances belonged to people recently killed.

Most of the chiefs and other people of importance who were known to the English during their former visit were still alive, and they met up with their old shipmate Oedidee. Captain Cook decided to leave Omai at Owharre, on the west side of the island of Huahaine, making the best terms with the chief that he could. The English were received on shore by a large gathering, many of whom seemed to be people of great importance, including a boy king. A ceremony took place, Omai making offerings to the gods, consisting of coloured feathers, cloths etc. Some of the chiefs also made offerings and a prayer dictated by Omai was said by a priest. Omai did not forget his friends in England, nor those who had brought him safely back. The King of England, Lord Sandwich, Cook and Clerke were mentioned in every one of them. Finally the chief agreed to give Omai a piece of ground extending about two hundred yards along the shore of the harbour and reaching up to the foot of a hill. A house was built for him to keep his European commodities in. On parting from Cook, Omai could not hold back his tears.

The ships entered the harbour of Ohamaneno on November 3rd, landing close into the shore, making an attempt to rid the ship of rats, with which they had become infested. Oreo, the chief of the island came to pay his respects to his old friend Cook. Friendly relations were threatened, however, by two incidents, one of which was the desertion of a marine, who, being on shore duty, went off carrying his weapon with him. Captain Cook, with a few of his men, immediately pursued him and he was soon found among the natives, who readily gave him up to the captain. A more serious case of desertion took place a few days later, being that of a midshipman and a seaman. The captain set off with two armed boats, but could not find the fugitives, learning that they had gone to the neighbouring island of Bolabola. The next morning, Oreo, his son and daughter, and his son-in-law, came on board the *Resolution,* and the last three mentioned were invited to the *Discovery,* with a view to detaining them until the deserters were brought back. As was to be expected, this high-handed act caused great consternation among the natives, who formed a plan to seize Cook while he was bathing, as was his custom every morning. Oreo had sent his canoes off to Bolabola and other places to try and find the deserters. Oreo, at length, set out for Bolabola, it being arranged that the ships should follow, but a strong wind kept them in the harbour. The next day Oreo returned with the two recreants, who had gone from Bolabola to the small island of Toobace, where they were taken by the father of Pootoe. Before leaving the island Cook presented Oreo with an English boar and sow and two goats. Oreo and several chiefs took passage on the English ships to Bolabola, where they were received by a great concourse of people with their great chief, Opoony, in their midst. As a ram had previously been conveyed to the island, Cook now made the present of a ewe to Opoony, hoping that the island may be stocked in time with a breed of sheep.

The ships then stood north, and on December 24th a small island with a lagoon was discovered. A large number of turtles were there and added to the food supply, but there was no fresh water. No traces of any inhabitants could be found either. Three hundred turtles were taken and as much fish as could be consumed. The telescopes were landed and on December 30th an eclipse of the sun was observed. Because they had spent Christmas there, Cook named it Christmas Island.

Leaving there on January 2nd,1778, the ships proceeded northwards. Although a large quantity of birds were seen, seeming to indicate the proximity of land, it was not until the 18th when first one high island came into sight, and then another, the first, being to windward, could not be approached. On standing towards the other, a third island was discovered. At first it was doubtful whether the islands were inhabited, but soon a number of canoes came alongside. the occupants would not come on board, but exchanged fish and some sweet potatoes for nails and other articles. They spoke the language of Tahiti and all wore a girdle, stained red, white and black, round the waist. As the ships sailed along the coast looking for an harbour, numerous villages were seen, with plantations of sugar-cane and plantains. Crowds gathered along the shore and on the heights to watch the ships. Several natives ventured on board, the next day, and showed by their wild looks and questions that they had not been visited by Europeans before. They did seem to know the value of iron and it was conjectured that they had gained their knowledge of it from the masts and spars of a ship with iron attached that had washed up on their shores. They soon showed themselves to be daring thieves, and on a boat being sent ashore, they attempted to steal the oars. They were fired at and one man was killed.

When Captain Cook landed, the natives fell flat on their faces. He understood that was the way they paid homage to their own chiefs. In his journal Cook expressed the belief that the people were cannibals. This came from seeing a man on board who had a piece of salted meat wrapped in a cloth, and which he said he ate to do him good. It seems to have been highly dried and seasoned, and eaten as a stimulant. The natives called their island Atooi, and Captain Cook gave the name of Sandwich Islands to the group, which we know today as the Hawaiian Islands.

Leaving the Sandwich Islands on February 2nd, the ships stood towards the coast of America until March 7th when the long-looked-for coast of New Albion, so called by Sir Francis Drake, hove into sight. The ships stood along the coast now off, now on again, with uncertain weather, until an inlet was found on March 29th. The ships sailed up the inlet for several miles, then anchored. Natives came off in three canoes shaped like Norwegian yawls. They made friendly gestures, strewing handfuls of red dust and feathers towards the explorers. Next day a large number came off with skins and furs for sale. The problem was finding articles to exchange for these valuable goods, for the natives would take nothing but metal, and at last insisted in only brass. To supply this, whole suits were stripped of their buttons, bureaux of their handles, and copper kettles, tin canisters and candlesticks went to wreck. The ships needed repairs, and even some new masts, so were hauled in close to the shore and securely moored. The natives called this inlet Nootka Sound, but Cook, true to style, gave it the name of King George's Sound.

Captain Cook kept to his intention to sail on April 26th, although the barometer fell very rapidly. Before long a great hurricane came on and the *Resolution* sprang a serious leak. When the weather moderated one pump kept it under control. As the ships passed along the coast, several islands and headlands were observed and named. One inlet, where the ships were brought up, was named Prince William's Sound. The natives here made a dam and attempted to plunder the *Discovery,* a number of them getting on board. Before they could achieve their object, the crew came on deck with their cutlasses, sending the plunderers off in their canoes.

Captain Cook, now believing that it was too late in the season to do anything in the way of new discoveries, decided to return to the south and wait at the Sandwich Islands until the next season. Leaving Prince William's Sound, the ships reached the island of Oonolaska. Some natives delivered two Russian letters, but these could not be understood. Soon after this the expedition suffered a great loss with the death of Mr Anderson, the surgeon of the *Resolution,* who had suffered for some time from tuberculosis.

On June 9th the ships anchored under a point of land which was believed to be the most western point of America, and to which was given the name of Cape Prince of Wales. It is only thirteen leagues distant from the eastern cape of Siberia, to which they next sailed to the county of Tschutski. On the 18th they fell in with ice as compact as a wall, and ten and twelve feet high, being much higher further to the north. It was covered with sea horses, some of which were caught and considered by many to be superior to salted pork. They continued to traverse the Arctic Sea beyond Bering Strait, until the 29th, when the ice beginning to form rapidly, Cook abandoned all hopes of achieving his object that year.

The ships anchored in the harbour of Samanoodha, in the island of Oonolaschka, on October 3rd. The carpenters were at once set to work repairing the ships. On the 14th a visit was made by a Russian of considerable ability to whom Cook entrusted a letter and chart for the Lord Commissioners of the Admiralty, which were duly delivered. The natives of this island were the best behaved of any yet met with, not one of them being guilty of an act of dishonesty , though their conduct was far from moral.

Leaving on October 20th, the ships proceeded south towards the Sandwich Islands, the commanders intention being to spend the winter there, and to return to Kamtschatska by the middle of May. The rigging of the ships had become very bad ; the *Discovery's* main-tack gave way, killed one man, and wounded the boatswain and two others.

On November 25th one of the Sandwich Islands, called by the natives Mowee [Maui], hove into view. Several canoes came off belonging to a chief called Terreeoboo ; but as another island was discovered, called

Owhyhee [Hawaii], which it was found possible to reach, the ships stood towards it, and their visitors accordingly left them. An eclipse of the moon was observed on December 2nd. For several weeks the ships plied round the island, bartering with the natives, who came off with hogs, fowls, fruit and roots. A bay was discovered on January 16th, 1779, and the masters were sent in to examine it, reporting back favourably, so next day the ships came to anchor in Kealakeua Bay.

The ships aroused great interest, being crowded with visitors. Natives lined the shore line, and many swan round the ships like shoals of fish. One rascally native stole the rudder out of a boat. Cook ordered some muskets and a four-pounder to be fired over the canoe, which was escaping.

Few of the voyagers now regretted that they had been unable to find a north-west passage home in the summer, as they (Captain Cook wrote) 'thus had it in their power to revisit the Sandwich Islands, and to enrich the voyage with a discovery which, though the last, seemed in many respects to be the most important that had hitherto been made by Europeans throughout the extent of the Pacific Ocean.'

Captain Cook found it necessary to take precautions against venereal disease, with which some of the crew were infected. He ruled, 'Such cases should not be allowed to go on shore, either as a duty, or for recreation, ' as he did not wish the disease to be transmitted to the natives.

The natives of Hawaii had a legend that a certain god, named Rono, or Orano, [some say Lono], formerly lived near Kealakeua Bay, and that, having killed his wife in a fit of jealousy, remorse drove him from the island. He set sail in a strangely shaped canoe, promising he would return on a floating island, furnished with all that man could desire. When, therefore the English ship appeared, their commander was thought to be the long-absent Rono. Much to Captain Cook's discomfort, every time he appeared on shore, the Hawaiians either fled in terror, or prostrated themselves before him. Several chiefs visited him, and the priests showed him their temple, or Morai, where he took part in a ceremony, and where, shortly after, he buried one of his old sailors who had died there. The native priests added their bit to the ceremony by throwing a dead hog and some plantains into the grave.

The attitude of the Hawaiians became gradually less friendly, some writers suggesting that Cook had interfered with their religious cycles, others that the economy of the island was suffering through supplying food to the crews. In any event, on February 4th the ships sailed, only to be shortly met with a hurricane, during which they picked up two canoes, driven off the land, the people in them nearly exhausted. A few days later they returned to Kealakeua Bay, but to a much less friendly reception than before, the bay being under taboo.[Sacred and forbidden]

Although many of the natives regarded him as a god, this had not stopped their thieving and one morning it was discovered that the *Discovery's* cutter had been stolen. When Lieutenant King boarded the *Resolution* at daylight, he found Captain Cook loading his double-barrelled gun. As he came on board the big guns of the ships were firing. Cook told him that he was going to take the king as an hostage, and that he had given orders to stop any canoes leaving the bay ; and to implement this the boats of both ships , well-manned and armed, were stationed across the bay. Cook landed with Lieutenant Philips and nine marines and immediately marched into the village and sought out the old king, Terreeboboo, who had just woken up. Cook informed him of the loss of the cutter and invited him to go aboard the *Resolution*. The king consented and would have gone willingly, but when they got to the boat, an old woman, who was one of the king's favourite wives, entreated him not to go. Two chiefs also came and took hold of the king, insisting that he go no further. The natives, fearful of the boats spread across the bay, began to crowd round the king, until, eventually, Cook gave up the point. What happened next is best told in the words of Lieutenant King :

'Though the enterprise which had led Captain Cook on shore had now failed, and was abandoned, yet his person did not seem to be in the least danger, till an accident happened, which gave a fatal turn to the affair. The boats, which had been stationed across the bay, having fired at some canoes that were attempting to get out, unfortunately had killed a chief of the first rank. The news of his death arrived at the village where Captain Cook was, just as he had left the king, and was walking slowly towards the shore. the ferment it occasioned was very conspicuous; the women and children were immediately sent off ; and the men put on their war-mats and armed themselves with sticks and stones. One of the natives, having in his hands a stone and a long iron spike (which they call a pahooa) came up to the captain, flourishing his weapon, by way of defiance and threatening to throw the stones. The captain desired him to desist ; but the man persisting in his insolence, he was at length provoked to firing a load of small shot.

THE DEATH OF CAPTAIN COOK.
From a painting by John Cleveley.

The man, having his mat on, which the shot was not able to penetrate, this had no other effect than to irritate and encourage them. Several stones were thrown at the marines, and one of the Erees attempted to stab Mr Philips with his pahooa, but failed in the attempt, and received from him a blow with the butt of his musket. Captain Cook now fired his second barrel, loaded with a ball, and killed one of the foremost of the natives. A general attack with stones immediately followed, which was answered by a discharge of musketry from the marines, and the people in the boats. The islanders, contrary to the expectations of everyone, stood the fire with great firmness ; and before the marines had time to reload, they broke in upon them with dreadful shouts and yells. What followed was a scene of the utmost horror and confusion.

'Four of the marines were cut off amongst the rocks in their retreat and fell a sacrifice to the fury of the enemy ; three more were dangerously wounded, and the lieutenant, who had received a stab between the shoulders with a pahooa, having fortunately reserved his fire, shot the man who had wounded him just as he was going to repeat his blow. Our unfortunate commander, the last time he was seen distinctly, was standing at the waters edge, and calling out to the boats to cease firing, and pull in. Having turned about to give his orders to the boats, he was stabbed in the back, and fell with his face into the water. On seeing him fall, the islanders set up a great shout, and his body was immediately dragged on shore, and surrounded by the enemy, who snatching the dagger from each others hands, showed a savage eagerness to have a share in his destruction.'

So fell the great commander in his fifty-first year, February 14th, 1779.

Lieutenant King went on shore to try and negotiate for the body of his former captain. It had been badly mutilated by the successive dagger blows, and was said to be in the possession of the king. On the 20th the hands and various parts of the body were brought on board, wrapped in a quantity of fine cloth, and covered with a cloak of black and white feathers. The feet and other parts were returned the next day, and being placed in a coffin they were committed to the deep, with the usual naval honours.

'Everyone on the ship was struck dumb and felt he had lost a father,' wrote one of the crew, ' The sad memories called forth on the day when we buried the fragments of his body in the sea caused all the crew to shed tears.'

Captain Clerke now succeeded to the command of the expedition, and removed to the *Resolution*. By him Mr Gore was appointed captain of the *Discovery*. Captain Clerke, although he was suffering from tuberculosis, resolved to try and find the north-west passage, but after getting fast in the arctic ice, had to give up. During the course of the voyage he died, when the command passed to Captain Gore, who took over the *Resolution*, while Captain King was given command of the *Discovery*.

After a long voyage and many adventures, the two ships arrived at the Nore on October 4th, 1780, after an absence of four years, two months and twenty-two days. These ships were certainly a tribute to their Whitby builders..

Captain King summed up Captain Cook's character as follows :

'The constitution of his body was robust, inured to labour, and capable of undergoing the severest hardships. His stomach bore. without difficulty, the coarsest and most ungrateful food. Indeed temperance in him was scarcely a virtue ; so great was the indifference with which he submitted to every kind of self-denial. The qualities of his mind were of the same hardy, vigorous kind whith those of his body. - His understanding was strong and perspicacious. His judgement, in whatever relative to the services he was engaging in, quick and sure. His designs were bold and manly ; and both in the conception, or in the mode of execution, bore evident marks of a great original genius. His courage was cool and determined, and accompanied with an admirable presence of mind in the moment of danger. His manners were plain and unaffected. His temper might perhaps have been justly blamed, as subject to hastiness and passion, had not these been disarmed by a disposition the most benevolent and humane.'

KING ARTHUR IN THE NORTH
A Study of This Renowned Historic Figure.

Keith Snowden

King Arthur - man or myth? Keith Snowden thinks there were two Arthurs; the one of the old romances and the war leader descended from the Romans.
His life and times, his campaigns and connections in the north of Britain are examined in this book

AUTHOR'S EDITION
ISBN 0 9527548 7 8

Price £2.85. Post 33p (Five or more copies post free).
AVAILABLE IN SOME LOCAL BOOKSHOPS OR DIRECT FROM THE PUBLISHER :
CASTLEDEN PUBLICATIONS, 11 Castlegate, Pickering, YO18 7AX. Telephone 01751-476227.

LOCAL & REGIONAL HISTORIES BY KEITH SNOWDEN

KINGS IN RYEDALE
Covers 2,000 years of Ryedales association with royalty.
A delightful volume of which he can be justifiably proud.
Nicholas Rhea, *Darlington & Stockton Times.*
AUTHOR'S FIRST EDITION. £1.95. Post 33p.

PICKERING THROUGH THE AGES, The Second Edition.
Now revised and enlarged, with extended text and many more pictures. Tells the story of the town from its foundation in pre-historic times to the present day.
£2.70. Post 44p. ISBN 0 9527548 2 7.

HELMSLEY & KIRKBY THROUGH THE AGES
Here is the story of these two ancient Yorkshire market towns and the many famous people connected with them.
£2.85. Post 44p. ISBN 0 9514657 4 0

MALTON & NORTON THROUGH THE AGES
The story of these ancient sister towns, their noble owners and famous sons.
REVISED EDITION. £2.85. Post 44p. ISBN 0 9514657 3 2

THORNTON DALE THROUGH THE AGES
Here is the story of one of Yorkshires prettiest villages and the famous people connected with it.
NEW EDITION £2.95. Post 44p. ISBN 0 9527548 6 X.

SCARBOROUGH THROUGH THE AGES
The story of the Queen of English Watering Places.
REVISED & ENLARGED EDITION.
£2.95. Post 44p. ISBN 0 9514657 9 1.

THE CIVIL WAR IN YORKSHIRE
An account of the battles and sieges and Yorkshires involvement. One of our best-sellers.
£2.95. Post 44p. ISBN 0 9514657 6 7.

WHITBY THROUGH THE AGES.
Pages from the history of this ancient Yorkshire sea port.
AUTHOR'S EDITION. £2.95. Post 44p.
ISBN 0 9527548 5 1.

KATHARINE PARR OUR NORTHERN QUEEN
The life and Northern associations of the last wife of King Henry VIII. A unique biography.
£2.95. Post 44p. ISBN 0 9514657 7 5.

MOORLAND MEMORIES
True tales from the Whitby and Pickering Moors.
AUTHOR'S EDITION. £2.85. Post 44p.
ISBN 0 9514657 8 3.

GREAT BATTLES IN YORKSHIRE
Recounting the many battles on Yorkshire soil from the Romans to the Roundheads.
NOW REPRINTED. £2.95. Post 44p.
ISBN 0 9527548 0 0.

HOUSE OF YORK AT WAR
A Yorkist account of the Wars of the Roses.
AUTHOR'S EDITION. £2.95. Post 44p.
ISBN 0 9527548 3 5

THE ADVENTUROUS CAPTAIN COOK
The life and voyages of James Cook, R.N.,F.R.S. Here is the life of this great Yorkshire-born navigator and his exciting voyages of discovery.
£2.99. Post 44p. ISBN 0 9527548 4 3.

KING ARTHUR IN THE NORTH
A study of this renowned historic figure.
AUTHOR'S EDITION £2.85. Post 44p.
ISBN 0 9527548 7 8.

ON SALE IN LOCAL BOOKSHOPS, OR DIRECT FROM THE PUBLISHER : CASTLEDEN PUBLICATIONS,
11 Castlegate, Pickering, North Yorkshire, YO18 7AX.
Telephone 01751 476227.
    Post free on five or more copies.